GUIDE TO METHODS

FOR STUDENTS OF

POLITICAL SCIENCE

STEPHEN VAN EVERA

GUIDE
TO
METHODS
FOR
STUDENTS
OF
POLITICAL
SCIENCE

Cornell University Press

ITHACA AND LONDON

First published 1997 by Cornell University Press
First printing, Cornell Paperbacks, 1997

Printed in the United States of America

Library of Congress Cataloging-in-Publication Data

Van Evera, Stephen,
Guide to methods for students of political science /
Stephen Van Evera
p.   cm.
Includes bibliographical references (p.   ).
ISBN-13: 978-0-8014-8457-5 (pbk. : alk. paper)
1. Political science—Methodology. I. Title.
JA71.V3   1997
320—DC21   97-17808

Cornell University Press strives to use environmentally responsible suppliers and materials to the fullest extent possible in the publishing of its books. Such materials include vegetable-based, low-VOC inks and acid-free papers that are recycled, totally chlorine-free, or partly composed of nonwood fibers. For further information, visit our website at www.cornellpress.cornell.edu.

Paperback printing   10   9   8

Contents

GUIDE TO METHODS
FOR STUDENTS OF
POLITICAL SCIENCE

Introduction

This book collects six papers that distill advice on methodology I have given, received, or overheard over the years. They address issues that get the most air time in classroom and hallway discussions in my neighborhood. I wrote them with graduate student readers in mind, but others may also find them useful. They began as how-to-do-it class handouts that I drafted to save me from further repeating oft-repeated advice. Any advice that I remembered giving more than once, however mundane ("Begin paragraphs with topic sentences!"), qualified for inclusion. At the same time I omitted standard advice that I rarely had to give.

Thus this book is not exhaustive or definitive. I make no effort to cover the methodological waterfront. (Main omission: I have no chapter on large-n study methods.)[1] All six chapters are basic

---

1. Many good primers on large-n methods have appeared, so my absent chapter will not be badly missed. I list some in Chapter 1, note 32. Also missing here are chapters on rational choice, critical, postmodern, and constructivist approaches. Friendly discussions of rational choice include Jon Elster, ed., *Rational Choice* (Oxford: Basil Blackwell, 1986), and Jeffrey Friedman, ed., *The Rational Choice Controversy* (New Haven: Yale University Press, 1996). Critical discussions include Donald P. Green and Ian Shapiro, *Pathologies of Rational Choice Theory: A Critique of Applications in Political Science* (New Haven: Yale University Press,

primers and state my personal viewpoint. None claims to summarize the views of the field or offer definitive answers. I wrote them less to promulgate solutions than to spur students to develop their own solutions to the puzzles the chapters address. The views expressed arise more from practicing methodology than studying it. They reflect my experience as a student, colleague, teacher, and editor. I learned some important things from writings on philosophy of science and social science methods, but I have found much of that writing abstruse and unuseful. It was often easier to invent my own answers than dig them up from the reams of muddy arcana produced by philosophers and methodologists, even when the answers existed somewhere in those reams.

This book reflects my field of concentration (international relations/security affairs). It focuses on concerns that are greater in the IR/security subfield (for example, the case-study method), and its examples are IR-heavy. I hope it nevertheless proves useful to students in other political science fields and in other social sciences. My regrets in advance to readers from these fields for its parochialisms—which stem from its origins as a collection of class handouts.

Chapter 1, "Hypotheses, Laws and Theories: A User's Guide,"

1994); Raymond E. Wolfinger, "The Rational Citizen Faces Election Day or What Rational Choice Theorists Don't Tell You about American Elections," in M. Kent Jennings and Thomas E. Mann, eds., *Elections at Home and Abroad* (Ann Arbor: University of Michigan Press, 1994), pp. 71–89; and Ashutosh Varshney, *Ethnic Conflict and Rational Choice: A Theoretical Engagement* (Cambridge: Center for International Affairs, Harvard University, Working Paper No. 95–11, 1995). Surveying critical, postmodern and constructivist approaches are Egon G. Guba and Yvonna S. Lincoln, "Competing Paradigms in Quantitative Research," in Norman K. Denzin and Yvonna S. Lincoln, eds., *Handbook of Qualitative Research* (Thousand Oaks, Calif.: Sage, 1994), pp. 105–17; Thomas A. Schwandt, "Constructivist, Interpretivist Approaches to Human Inquiry," in Denzin and Lincoln, *Handbook*, pp. 118–37; and Joe L. Kincheloe and Peter L. McLaren, "Rethinking Critical Theory and Qualitative Research," in Denzin and Lincoln, *Handbook*, pp. 138–57.

began as a three-page handout on scientific inference for an undergraduate class I taught at U.C. Davis many years ago. Finding no primer that explained how to frame, assess, and apply theories, I wrote my own. It expanded over the years and reflects my own barefoot positivist, anti-obfuscationist viewpoint. I am unpersuaded by the view that the prime rules of scientific method should differ between "hard science" and the social sciences. Science is science. I also believe the basic rules of science, often complexified, are actually few in number and can be plainly stated and briefly summarized.

The subjects of Chapter 1—the basic tools and rules of scientific inference—are often skipped over in the methods texts. Much writing on social science methods assumes that readers already know what theories are, what good theories are, what elements theories contain, how theories should be expressed, what fundamental rules should be followed when testing or applying theories, and so on. This chapter stresses the elementary points others omit.

Chapter 2, "What Are Case Studies? How Should They Be Performed?" began as a graduate class handout drafted to escort an assignment to produce a short case study. Finding no short primer on how to do case studies, I wrote my own. I intended it as a starting point for students with no exposure to the case method.

Case study is the poor cousin among social science methods. The mainstream methodology literature pays vast attention to large-n methods while dismissing case methods with a wave. Many political science graduate programs teach large-n methods as the only technique: "methodology" classes cover large-n methods (or large-n and rational choice) as if these were all there is. Case-study methods are seldom taught and are almost never taught in a class of their own. (Exceptions include classes on the case method taught by Stephen Walt and John Mearsheimer at the University of Chicago, by Scott Sagan at Stanford, by Peter Liberman at Tulane, by Andy Bennett at Georgetown, by Ted Hopf at the University of Michigan, and by John Odell at the University of Southern California.)

I regard large-n and case-study methods as essential equals. Each has its strengths and weaknesses. Sometimes one is the stronger method, sometimes the other. Hence the imbalanced attention they receive should be righted. The fault for this imbalance lies partly with case-study practitioners themselves, however. They have not produced a simple how-to cookbook for novices. With no cookbook that distills the method others are bound to neglect it. I wrote this chapter as a first cut toward such a cookbook.

Chapter 3, "What Is a Political Science Dissertation?" reflects my view that we often define the boundaries of the field too narrowly. A wider range of thesis topics and formats should be considered fair game. Specifically, political science field culture is biased toward the creation and testing of theory over other work, including the application of theory to solve policy problems and answer historical questions and the stock-taking of literature. But making and testing theories are not the only games in town. Applying theories to evaluate past and present policies and to solve historical puzzles is also worth doing. If everyone makes and tests theories but no one ever uses them, then what are they for? Theorizing is pointless if we never apply our theories to solve problems. Stock-taking work is also growing more valuable as our literature expands to the point where no one can take stock of the whole on their own.

Moreover, theory-making and theory-testing can be tall orders for scholars at the beginning of their careers. Grand theorizing takes time to learn, and applying theories or taking stock can be a more feasible way to start. Theory-application and stock-taking both require good facility with theories, and both allow wide latitude to demonstrate that facility with less risk of utter failure. Hence dissertations of this genre should be recognized as respectable social science and considered as alternatives when grand-theory options look daunting.

Chapter 3 also reflects my view that political science should embrace the task of historical explanation among its missions. Historians should not be left alone with the assignment. Many historians are leery of generalizations, hence of the use of general theories; yet theories are essential to historical explanation. Many are averse to explicit explanation, instead preferring to "let the facts speak for themselves." Many are averse to writing evaluative history that judges policies and policymakers. Political science should step in to fill the explanatory and evaluative gaps that are left by these quirks in historian culture.

Chapters 4 and 5, "Helpful Hints on Writing a Political Science Dissertation" and "The Dissertation Proposal," distill craft advice that I have given to students and colleagues over the years, and that others have given to me. They focus on questions of presentation and on broader questions of academic strategy and tactics, while slighting the (usually more important) question of research design. In part they reflect my time editing *International Security* and the many discussions I had about writing and presentation with *IS* readers and authors.

Chapter 6, "Professional Ethics," is somewhat off the narrow methodological point of the others, but it does touch methodology in a large sense by asking: how should we work together as a community? It reflects my feeling that the social sciences need some formal discussion of professional ethics. Social science operates largely beyond accountability to others. Institutions and professions that face weak accountability need inner ethical rudders that define their obligations in order to say on course. Otherwise they risk straying into parasitic disutility. Social science is no exception.

I include an appendix, "How to Write a Paper," with the thought that teachers might find it a useful class handout. It distills my advice to undergraduates on writing class papers. What should a short paper look like? These are my suggestions. I give it to classes along with all paper assignments.

For educating me on many matters discussed here I thank Robert Arseneau, with whom I discussed many of these issues while he taught PS3 at U.C. Berkeley. For comments on these chapters and/or these issues I also thank Steve Ansolabehere, Bob Art, Andy Bennett, Tom Christensen, Alex George, Charlie Glaser, Chaim Kaufmann, Peter Liberman, John Mearsheimer, Bill Rose, Scott Sagan, Jack Snyder, Marc Trachtenberg, Steve Walt, Sandy Weiner, and David Woodruff. I also thank the many teachers, students, and colleagues who have commented on my work through the years. Much of what I offer here is recycled advice they once gave me.

Hypotheses, Laws, and Theories: A User's Guide

What Is a Theory?

Definitions of the term "theory" offered by philosophers of social science are cryptic and diverse.[1] I recommend the following as a simple framework that captures their main meaning while also spelling out elements they often omit.

Theories are general statements that describe and explain the

---

1. Most posit that theories explain phenomena and leave it at that. The elements of an explanation are not detailed. See, for example, Brian Fay and J. Donald Moon, "What Would an Adequate Philosophy of Social Science Look Like?" in Michael Martin and Lee C. McIntyre, eds., *Readings in the Philosophy of Social Science* (Cambridge: MIT Press, 1994), p. 26: a social theory is a "systematic, unified explanation of a diverse range of social phenomena." Likewise Earl Babbie, *The Practice of Social Research*, 7th ed. (Belmont, Calif.: Wadsworth, 1995), p. 40: "A theory is a systematic explanation for the observations that relate to a particular aspect of life." See also Kenneth Waltz, quoted in note 9. Each leaves the components of an explanation unspecified.

Leaving even explanation unmentioned is W. Phillips Shively, *The Craft of Political Research*, 3d ed. (Englewood Cliffs, N.J.: Prentice-Hall, 1990): "A theory takes a set of similar things that happen—say, the development of party systems in democracies—and finds a common pattern among them that allows us to treat each of these different occurrences as a repeated example of the same thing" (p. 2).

causes or effects of classes of phenomena. They are composed of causal laws or hypotheses, explanations, and antecedent conditions. Explanations are also composed of causal laws or hypotheses, which are in turn composed of dependent and independent variables. Fourteen definitions bear mention:

law

> An observed regular relationship between two phenomena. Laws can be deterministic or probabilistic. The former frame invariant relationships ("if A then always B"). The latter frame probabilistic relationships ("if A then sometimes B, with probability X"). Hard science has many deterministic laws. Nearly all social science laws are probabilistic.
>
> Laws can be causal ("A causes B") or noncausal ("A and B are caused by C; hence A and B are correlated but neither causes the other").[2] Our prime search is for causal laws. We explore the possibility that laws are noncausal mainly to rule it out, so we can rule in the possibility that observed laws are causal.[3]

2. Generic laws (which might be causal or noncausal) should be stated in associative language ("if A, then B," or "the greater A, the greater B", or "the higher A, the smaller B", etc.). Causal laws can also be framed with causal language ("A causes B").

3. Causal laws can assume four basic causal patterns: direct causation ("A causes B"), reverse causation ("B causes A"), reciprocal causation ("A causes B and B causes A"), and self-undermined causation ("A causes B and B lessens A"). Hypotheses, discussed below, can assume the same formats. To establish a specific causal relationship ("A causes B"), we must rule out the possibility that an observed relationship between A and B is spurious ("C causes A and B") or reverse-causal ("B causes A"). We may also investigate whether reciprocal causation or self-undermined causation is at work.

hypothesis	A conjectured relationship between two phenomena.[4] Like laws, hypotheses can be of two types: causal ("I surmise that A causes B") and noncausal ("I surmise that A and B are caused by C; hence A and B are correlated but neither causes the other").
theory	A causal law ("I have established that A causes B") or a causal hypothesis ("I surmise that A causes B"), together with an explanation of the causal law or hypothesis that explicates how A causes B. Note: the term "general theory" is often used for more wide-ranging theories, but all theories are by definition general to some degree.
explanation	The causal laws or hypotheses that connect the cause to the phenomenon being caused, showing how causation occurs. ("A causes B because A causes q, which causes r, which causes B.")
antecedent condition[5]	A phenomenon whose presence activates or

4. This follows P. McC. Miller and M. J. Wilson, *A Dictionary of Social Science Methods* (New York: John Wiley, 1983), p. 58: "[A hypothesis is] a conjecture about the relationships between two or more concepts." Carl Hemple uses "hypothesis" more broadly, to include conjectures about facts as well as relationships. Thus, for Hempel, descriptive conjectures (for instance, estimates of the height of the Empire State Building or the size of the national debt) are also hypotheses. See Carl G. Hempel, *Philosophy of Natural Science* (Englewood Cliffs, N.J.: Prentice-Hall, 1966), p. 19. I use the term "propositions" to refer to what Hempel calls "hypotheses": thus, for me, propositions can be hypotheses or descriptive conjectures. Babbie, *Practice of Social Research*, also uses "hypothesis" broadly (see p. 49); under "hypothesis" he includes predictions inferred from hypotheses (which I call "predictions," "observable implications," or "test implications" of theory).
5. The term is from Carl G. Hempel, *Aspects of Scientific Explanation and Other Essays in the Philosophy of Science* (New York: Free Press, 1965), pp. 246–47 and passim. The term "antecedent" merely means that the condition's presence pre-

magnifies the action of a causal law or hypothesis. Without it causation operates more weakly ("*A* causes some *B* if *C* is absent, more *B* if *C* is present"—e.g., "Sunshine makes grass grow, but causes large growth only in fertilized soil") or not at all ("*A* causes *B* if *C* is present, otherwise not"— e.g., "Sunshine makes grass grow, but only if we also get some rainfall").

We can restate an antecedent condition as a causal law or hypothesis. ("*C* causes *B* if *A* is present, otherwise not"—e.g., "Rainfall makes grass grow, but only if we also get some sunshine").

Antecedent conditions are also called "interaction terms," "initial conditions," "enabling conditions," "catalytic conditions," "preconditions," "activating conditions," "magnifying conditions," "assumptions," "assumed conditions," or "auxiliary assumptions."

variable   A concept that can have various values, e.g., the "degree of democracy" in a country or the "share of the two-party vote" for a political party.

independent variable (IV)   A variable framing the causal phenomenon of a causal theory or hypothesis. In the hypothesis "literacy causes democracy," the degree of literacy is the independent variable.

---

cedes the causal process that it activates or magnifies. Antecedent conditions need not precede the arrival of the independent variable onto the scene; they can appear after the appearance of high values on the independent variable that they activate or magnify.

dependent variable (DV)	A variable framing the caused phenomenon of a causal theory or hypothesis. In the hypothesis "literacy causes democracy," the degree of democracy is the dependent variable.
intervening variable (IntV)	A variable framing intervening phenomenon included in a causal theory's explanation. Intervening phenomena are caused by the IV and cause the DV.[6] In the theory "Sunshine causes photosynthesis, causing grass to grow," photosynthesis is the intervening variable.
condition variable (CV)[7]	A variable framing an antecedent condition. The values of condition variables govern the size of the impact that IVs or IntVs have on DVs and other IntVs. In the hypothesis "Sunshine makes grass grow, but only if we also get some rainfall," the amount of rainfall is a condition variable.
study variable (SV)	A variable whose causes or effects we seek to discover with our research. A project's study variable can be an IV, DV, IntV, or CV.
prime hypothesis	The overarching hypothesis that frames the relationship between a theory's independent and dependent variables.

6. Whether a specific variable is dependent, independent, or intervening depends on its context and changes with context, as with A in these statements: (1) "A causes B": A is the independent variable; (2) "Q causes A": A becomes the dependent variable; and (3) "Q causes A, and A causes B": A becomes an intervening variable.

7. Condition variables are also known as "suppressor" variables, meaning that controlling values on these variables suppresses irregular variance between independent and dependent variables. See Miller and Wilson, *Dictionary of Social Science Methods*, p. 110.

explanatory hypothesis | The intermediate hypotheses that constitute a theory's explanation.[8]
test hypothesis | The hypothesis we seek to test. Also called the "research hypothesis."

Note: a theory, then, is nothing more than a set of connected causal laws or hypotheses.[9]

We can always "arrow-diagram" theories, like this:

$$A \rightarrow q \rightarrow r \rightarrow B$$

In this diagram A is the theory's independent variable, B is the dependent variable. The letters q and r indicate intervening vari-

8. These last four terms—"condition variable," "study variable," "prime hypothesis," and "explanatory hypothesis"—are my own nominations to fill word-gaps in the lexicon.
9. For a different view see Kenneth N. Waltz, *Theory of International Politics* (Reading, Mass.: Addison-Wesley, 1979), pp. 2, 5. To Waltz, theories are not "mere collections of laws" but rather the "statements that explain them" (p. 5). These statements include "theoretical notions," which can take the form of concepts or assumptions. I prefer my definition to Waltz's because all explanations for social science laws that I find satisfying can be reduced to laws or hypotheses. His definition of "explanation" also lacks precision because it leaves the prime elements of an explanation unspecified.
For a third meaning, more restrictive than mine, see Christopher H. Achen and Duncan Sindal, "Rational Deterrence Theory and Comparative Case Studies," *World Politics* 41 (January 1989): 147: A theory is "a very general set of propositions from which others, including 'laws,' are derived." Their definition omits modestly general ideas that I call theories.
Nearer my usage is Carl Hempel: "Theories . . . are bodies of systematically related hypotheses." Carl G. Hempel, "The Function of General Laws in History," in Martin and McIntyre, *Readings in the Philosophy of Social Science*, p. 49. Likewise Miller and Wilson, *Dictionary of Social Science Methods*: "[A theory is] a set of integrated hypotheses designed to explain particular classes of events" (p. 112). Similar are Gary King, Robert O. Keohane, and Sidney Verba, *Designing Social Inquiry: Scientific Inference in Qualitative Research* (Princeton: Princeton University Press, 1994), p. 99: "Causal theories are designed to show the causes of a phenomenon or set of phenomena" and include "an interrelated set of causal hypotheses. Each hypothesis specifies a posited relationship between variables."

ables and comprise the theory's explanation. The proposal "$A \rightarrow B$" is the theory's prime hypothesis, while the proposals that "$A \rightarrow q$," "$q \rightarrow r$," and "$r \rightarrow B$" are its explanatory hypotheses.

We can add condition variables, indicating them by using the multiplication symbol, "×."[10] Here C is a condition variable: the impact of A on q is magnified by a high value on C and reduced by a low value on C.

$$A \rightarrow q \rightarrow r \rightarrow B$$
$$\times$$
$$C$$

An example would be:

Amount of sunshine		Amount of photosynthesis		Amount of grass growth
×				
Amount of rainfall				

sunshine $\rightarrow$ photosynthesis $\rightarrow$ grass growth

One can display a theory's explanation at any level of detail. Here I have elaborated the link between r and B to show explanatory variables s and t.

$$A \rightarrow q \rightarrow r \rightarrow s \rightarrow t \rightarrow B$$
$$\times$$
$$C$$

One can extend an explanation to define more remote causes. Here remote causes of A (Y and Z) are detailed:

10. The multiplication sign is used here only to indicate that the CV magnifies the impact of the IV, not to mean that the CV literally multiplies the impact of the IV (although it might).

$$Y \rightarrow Z \rightarrow A \rightarrow q \rightarrow r \rightarrow s \rightarrow t \rightarrow B$$
$$\times$$
$$C$$

We can detail the causes of condition variables, as here with the cause of *C:*

$$Y \rightarrow Z \rightarrow A \rightarrow q \rightarrow r \rightarrow s \rightarrow t \rightarrow B$$
$$\times$$
$$X \rightarrow C$$

There is no limit to the number of antecedent conditions we can frame. Here more conditions (*D, u, v*) are specified.

$$Y \rightarrow Z \rightarrow A \rightarrow q \rightarrow r \rightarrow s \rightarrow t \rightarrow B$$
$$\times \qquad\qquad \times$$
$$X \rightarrow C \qquad\qquad u$$
$$\times \qquad\qquad \times$$
$$D \qquad\qquad v$$

One can add more avenues of causation between causal and caused variables. Here two chains of causation between *A* and *B* (running through intervening variables *f* and *g*) are added, to produce a three-chain theory:

$$\rightarrow \rightarrow \rightarrow \rightarrow \rightarrow \rightarrow \rightarrow f \rightarrow$$
$$Y \rightarrow Z \rightarrow A \rightarrow \rightarrow \rightarrow \rightarrow \rightarrow \rightarrow \rightarrow g \rightarrow B$$
$$\rightarrow q \rightarrow r \rightarrow s \rightarrow t \rightarrow$$
$$\times \qquad\qquad \times$$
$$X \rightarrow C \qquad\qquad u$$
$$\times \qquad\qquad \times$$
$$D \qquad\qquad v$$

A "theory" that cannot be arrow-diagrammed *is not a theory* and needs reframing to become a theory. (According to this criteria much political science "theory" and "theoretical" writing is not theory.)

What Is a Specific Explanation?

Explanations of specific events (particular wars, revolutions, election outcomes, economic depressions, and so on) use theories and are framed like theories. A good explanation tells us what specific causes produced a specific phenomenon and identifies the general phenomenon of which this specific cause is an example. Three concepts bear mention:

specific explanation	An explanation cast in specific terms that accounts for a distinctive event. Like a theory, it describes and explains cause and effect, but these causes and effects are framed in singular terms. (Thus "expansionism causes aggression, causing war" is a theory; "German expansionism caused German aggression, causing World War II" is a specific explanation.) Specific explanations are also called "particular explanations" (as opposed to "general explanations.")

Specific explanations come in two types. The second type ("generalized specific explanation") is more useful:

nongeneralized specific explanation	A specific explanation that does not identify the theory that the operating cause is an example of. ("Germany caused World War II." The explanation does not answer the ques-

	tion "of what is Germany an example?")[11]
generalized specific explanation	A specific explanation that identifies the theories that govern its operation.[12] ("German expansionism caused World War II." The operating cause, "German expansionism," is an example of expansionism, which is the independent variable in the hypothesis "expansionism causes war.")

Specific explanations are composed of causal, caused, intervening, and antecedent phenomena:[13]

causal phenomenon (CP)	The phenomenon doing the causing.
caused phenomenon (OP)	The phenomenon being caused.
intervening phenomena (IP)	Phenomena that form the explanation's explanation. These are caused by the causal phenomenon and cause the outcome phenomenon.
antecedent phenomena (AP)	Phenomena whose presence activates or magnifies the causal action of the causal and/or explanatory phenomena.[14]

11. Such explanations rest on implicit theories, however, as Carl Hempel has explained. See Hempel, "Function of General Laws in History."
12. The theories thus identified are sometimes termed the "warrants" of the argument or explanation. See Wayne C. Booth, Gregory G. Colomb, and Joseph M. Williams, *The Craft of Research* (Chicago: University of Chicago Press, 1995), pp. 90–92, 111–31. "The warrant of an argument is its general principle, an assumption or premise that bridges the claim and its supporting evidence" (ibid., p. 90).
13. Specific explanations are composed of singular phenomena that represent specific values on variables, not of variables themselves. As such they are "phenomena," not "variables." On assessing specific explanations see "How Can Specific Events Be Explained," in this chapter.
14. These last seven terms—"specific explanation," "nongeneralized specific explanation," "generalized specific explanation," "causal phenomenon," "caused phenomenon," "intervening phenomenon," and "antecedent phenomenon"—

We arrow-diagram specific explanations the same way we do theories:

A theory	Expansionism → Aggression → War
A generalized specific explanation	German expansionism → German aggression → World War II
A nongeneralized specific explanation	Germany → Outbreak of fighting on September 1, 1939 → World War II

What Is a Good Theory?

Seven prime attributes govern a theory's quality.
1. A good theory has *large explanatory power*. The theory's independent variable has a large effect on a wide range of phenomena under a wide range of conditions. Three characteristics govern explanatory power:
   Importance. Does variance in the value on the independent variable cause large or small variance in the value on the dependent variable?[15] An important theory points to a cause that has a large impact—one that causes large variance on the dependent vari-

---

are my suggested labels for these concepts. Others use "explanandum phenomenon" for the caused phenomenon, and "explanans" for a generalized explanation and its components (the causal, intervening, and antecedent phenomena). See, for example, Hempel, *Philosophy of Natural Science*, p. 50. (In Hempel's usage only generalized specific explanations comprise an explanans—nongeneralized specific explanation do not.)

15. A theory's importance can be measured in "theoretical" or "dispersion" terms. A theoretical measure of importance asks: how many units of change in the value on the dependent variable are caused by a unit of change in the value on the independent variable? (How many additional votes can a candidate gain by spending an additional campaign dollar on television ads?) A dispersion measure asks: what share of the DV's total variance in a specific data set is caused by variance of this IV? (What percentage of the variance in the votes received by various congressional candidates is explained by variance in their television spending?) I use "importance" in the former sense, to refer to theoretical importance. See Christopher H. Achen, *Interpreting and Using Regression* (Beverly Hills: Sage, 1982), pp. 68–77.

able. The greater the variance produced, the greater the theory's explanatory power.

Explanatory range. How many classes of phenomena does variance in the value on the theory's independent variable affect, hence explain? The wider the range of affected phenomena, the greater the theory's explanatory power. Most social science theories have narrow range, but a few gems explain many diverse domains.[16]

Applicability. How common is the theory's cause in the real world? How common are antecedent conditions that activate its operation? The more prevalent the causes and conditions of the theory, the greater its explanatory power.[17] The prevalence of

16. Karl Deutsch used the terms "combinatorial richness" and "organizing power" for attributes similar to what I call explanatory range, with "combinatorial richness" expressing "the range of combinations or patterns that can be generated from" a model, and "organizing power" defining the correspondence of the theory or model to phenomena other than those it was first used to explain. Karl Deutsch, *The Nerves of Government* (New York: Free Press, 1966), pp. 16–18. Examples of social science theories with wide explanatory range include Mancur Olson's theory of public goods, Robert Jervis's offense-defense theory of war and arms racing, Stanislav Andreski's military-participation ratio (MPR) explanation for social stratification, and Stephen Walt's balance-of-threat theory of alliances. See Mancur Olson, *The Logic of Collective Action* (Cambridge: Harvard University Press, 1971); Robert Jervis, "Cooperation under the Security Dilemma," *World Politics* 30 (January 1978): 167–214; Stanislav Andreski, *Military Organization and Society* (Berkeley: University of California Press, 1971), pp. 20–74; and Stephen M. Walt, *The Origins of Alliances* (Ithaca: Cornell University Press, 1987), pp. 17–33.

17. Even causes that produce powerful effects can have little explanatory power if these causes are rare in the real world, or if they require rare antecedent conditions to operate. Conversely, causes that produce weaker effects can have greater explanatory power if the cause and its antecedent conditions are common. Thus great white shark attacks are often lethal, but they explain few deaths because they are scarce in the real world. The cause is strong but rare, hence it explains little. Sunburn is less lethal but explains more death (through skin cancer) because it is more common. Likewise, scuba diving is often lethal if hungry great white sharks are around, but scuba diving explains few deaths because divers avoid shark-infested waters. The cause is powerful under the right conditions (hungry sharks nearby), but these conditions are rare, hence the cause explains few events. Sunburn explains more deaths because it does not require rare conditions to produce its harmful effects.

these causes and conditions in the past govern its power to explain history. Their current and future prevalence govern its power to explain present and future events.

2. Good theories elucidate by simplifying. Hence a good theory is *parsimonious*. It uses few variables simply arranged to explain its effects.

Gaining parsimony often requires some sacrifice of explanatory power, however. If that sacrifice is too large it becomes unworthwhile. We can tolerate some complexity if we need it to explain the world.

3. A good theory is "*satisfying*," that is, it satisfies our curiosity. A theory is unsatisfying if it leaves us wondering what causes the cause proposed by the theory. This happens when theories point to familiar causes whose causes, in turn, are a mystery. A politician once explained her election loss: "I didn't get enough votes!" This is true but unsatisfying. We still want to know why she didn't get enough votes.

The further removed a cause stands from its proposed effect, the more satisfying the theory. Thus "droughts cause famine" is less satisfying than "changes in ocean surface temperature cause shifts in atmospheric wind patterns, causing shifts in areas of heavy rainfall, causing droughts, causing famine."

4. A good theory is *clearly framed*. Otherwise we cannot infer predictions from it, test it, or apply it to concrete situations.

A clearly framed theory fashions its variables from concepts that the theorist has clearly defined.

A clearly framed theory includes a full outline of the theory's explanation. It does not leave us wondering how *A* causes *B*. Thus "changes in ocean temperature cause famine" is less complete than "changes in ocean temperature cause shifts in atmospheric wind patterns, causing shifts in areas of heavy rainfall, causing droughts, causing famine."

A clearly framed theory includes a statement of the antecedent conditions that enable its operation and govern its impact. Otherwise we cannot tell what cases the theory governs and thus cannot infer useful policy prescriptions.

Foreign policy disasters often happen because policymakers apply valid theories to inappropriate circumstances. Consider the hypothesis that "appeasing other states makes them more aggressive, causing war." This was true with Germany during 1938–39, but the opposite is sometimes true: a firm stand makes the other more aggressive, causing war. To avoid policy backfires, therefore, policymakers must know the antecedent conditions that decide if a firm stand will make others more or less aggressive. Parallel problems arise in all policymaking domains and highlight the importance of framing antecedent conditions clearly.

5. A good theory is in principle *falsifiable*. Data that would falsify the theory can be defined (although it may not now be available).[18]

Theories that are not clearly framed may be nonfalsifiable because their vagueness prevents investigators from inferring predictions from them.

Theories that make omnipredictions that are fulfilled by all observed events are also nonfalsifiable. Empirical tests cannot corroborate or infirm such theories because all evidence is consistent with them. Religious theories of phenomena have this quality: happy outcomes are God's reward, disasters are God's punishment, cruelties are God's tests of our faith, and outcomes that elude these broad categories are God's mysteries. Some Marxist arguments share this omni-predictional trait.[19]

6. A good theory *explains important phenomena*: it answers ques-

18. Discussing this requirement of theory is Hempel, *Philosophy of Natural Science*, pp. 30–32.
19. For other examples see King, Keohane, and Verba, *Designing Social Inquiry*, p. 113, mentioning Talcott Parsons's theory of action and David Easton's systems' analysis of macropolitics. On Easton see also Harry Eckstein, "Case Study and Theory in Political Science," in Fred I. Greenstein and Nelson W. Polsby, eds., *Handbook of Political Science*, vol. 7, *Strategies of Inquiry* (Reading, Mass.: Addison-Wesley, 1975), p. 90.

tions that matter to the wider world, or it helps others answer such questions. Theories that answer unasked questions are less useful even if they answer these questions well. (Much social science theorizing has little real-world relevance and thus fails this test.)

7. A good theory has *prescriptive richness*. It yields useful policy recommendations.

A theory gains prescriptive richness by pointing to manipulable causes, since manipulable causes might be controlled by human action. Thus "capitalism causes imperialism, causing war" is less useful than "offensive military postures and doctrines cause war," even if both theories are equally valid, because the structure of national economies is less manipulable than national military postures and doctrines. "Teaching chauvinist history in school causes war" is even more useful, since the content of national education is more easily adjusted than national military policy.

A theory gains prescriptive richness by identifying dangers that could be averted or mitigated by timely countermeasures. Thus theories explaining the causes of hurricanes provide no way to prevent them, but they do help forecasters warn threatened communities to secure property and take shelter.

A theory gains prescriptive richness by identifying antecedent conditions required for its operation (see point 4). The better these conditions are specified the greater our ability to avoid misapplying the theory's prescriptions to situations that the theory does not govern.

How Can Theories Be Made?

There is no generally accepted recipe for making theories.[20] Some scholars use deduction, inferring explanations from more

20. Arguing the impossibility of a recipe is Hempel, *Philosophy of Natural Science*, pp. 10–18. Also see Milton Friedman, *Essays in Positive Economics* (Chicago: University of Chicago Press, 1953): constructing hypotheses "is a creative act of inspiration, intuition, invention . . . the process must be discussed in psychologi-

general, already-established causal laws. Thus much economic theory is deduced from the assumption that people seek to maximize their personal economic utility. Others make theories inductively: they look for relationships between phenomena; then they investigate to see if discovered relationships are causal; then they ask "of what more general causal law is this specific cause-effect process an example?" For example, after observing that clashing efforts to gain secure borders helped cause the Arab-Israeli wars, a theorist might suggest that competition for security causes war.[21]

Nine aids to theory-making bear mention. (The first eight are inductive, the last is deductive.)

1. We can examine "outlier" cases, that is, cases poorly explained by existing theories.[22] Unknown causes must explain their outcomes. We try to identify these causes by examining the case.

Specifically, to make a new theory we select cases where the phenomenon we seek to explain is abundant but its known causes are scarce or absent. Unknown causes must be at work. These causes will announce themselves as unusual characteristics of the case and as phenomena that are associated with the dependent variable within the case. We nominate these phenomena as candidate causes.[23] We also cull the views of people who experienced

cal, not logical, categories; studied in autobiographies and biographies, not treatises on scientific method; and promoted by maxim and example, not syllogism or theorem" (p. 43). On the subject of theory-making see also Shively, *Craft of Political Research,* pp. 163–66, where Shively notes the possibility of creating theories by induction, deduction, and borrowing theories from other fields.

21. From there the theorist could move further by returning to deduction, for instance, deducing that conditions that intensify competition for security—such as an advantage for the offensive on the battlefield—are also causes of war.

22. Such cases lie furthest from the regression line expressing the relationship between the dependent variable and its known causes; hence the term "outlier" cases. Another term for exploring outlier cases is "deviant-case analysis." See Arend Lijphart, "Comparative Politics and the Comparative Method," *American Political Science Review* 65 (September 1971): 692.

23. For example, India is a democracy with a low level of public literacy. Literacy

the case or know it well and nominate their explanations as candidate causes.

To infer a theory's antecedent conditions (CVs), we select cases where the dependent variable's causes are abundant but the dependent variable is scarce or absent. This suggests that unknown antecedent conditions are absent in the case. Study of the case may identify them.

2. The "method of difference" and "method of agreement" (proposed by John Stuart Mill)[24] can serve as aids to inductive theory-making. In the method of difference the analyst compares cases with similar background characteristics and different values on the study variable (that is, the variable whose causes or effects we seek to discover), looking for other differences between cases. We nominate these other cross-case differences as possible causes of the study variable (if we seek to discover its causes) or its possible effects (if we seek its effects). We pick similar cases to reduce the number of candidate causes or effects that emerge: the more similar the cases, the fewer the candidates, making real causes and effects easier to spot.[25] Likewise, in the method of

---

is an established cause of democracy, hence India is an "outlier" case, falling far from the regression line expressing the relationship between degree of democracy (the dependent variable) and levels of literacy (the independent variable). Exploring the India case will uncover causes of democracy that operate independently of literacy and in addition to it.

24. John Stuart Mill, *A System of Logic*, ed. J. M. Robson (Toronto: University of Toronto Press, 1973), chap. 8, "Of the Four Methods of Experimental Inquiry," pp. 388–406.

25. An example of using paired method-of-difference case studies for theory-making is Morris P. Fiorina, *Congress: Keystone of the Washington Establishment* (New Haven: Yale University Press, 1977), chap. 4, pp. 29–37. Fiorina sought to explain why marginal congressional districts ("swing" districts where Democrats and Republicans compete evenly in congressional elections) were disappearing. To generate hypotheses he compared two districts highly similar in character but different in result: one district had always been and remained marginal, the other had changed from marginal to nonmarginal during the 1960s. He nominated the key cross-district difference that he observed (greater constituent servicing by the congressional incumbent in the newly nonmarginal

agreement the analyst explores cases with different characteristics and similar values on the study variable, looking for other similarities between the cases, and nominating these similarities as possible causes or effects of the variable.[26]

3. We can select cases with extreme high or low values on the

---

district) as a possible cause of the general decline of marginality. The growth of government, he theorized, had created opportunities for incumbents to win the voters' favor by performing constituent service, and this bolstered incumbents who seized the opportunity.

I also had an early social science adventure inferring a hypothesis by method-of-difference case comparison (although I was oblivious of J. S. Mill at the time). In 1969 I sought to explain why black political mobilization remained low in the rural Deep South even after the passage of the 1965 Voting Rights Act. I inferred an explanation—holding that economic coercion by whites was retarding black mobilization—partly from Delphi-method interviews (see note 27) but also from a method-of-difference comparison.

I started by comparing two very similar black-majority Mississippi counties. Holmes and Humphries counties were virtual twins on nearly all socioeconomic dimensions except one: blacks had won county-wide elections in Holmes but lost badly in next-door Humphries. This spurred my search for a second difference between them. It was easy to spot. Holmes had the Mileston project, a community of black landowners who bought small farms through the New Deal Farm Security Administration in the 1940s. Humphries had nothing similar. As a result Holmes had far more black landowners than Humphries. Further investigation (process tracing) revealed that these landowners had played a key role in building Holmes County's black political organization. Interviews further suggested that fear of eviction among black tenant farmers deterred their political participation throughout Mississippi, and the Mileston farmers were emboldened to participate by their freedom from fear of eviction. A large-n test using all twenty-nine black-majority Mississippi counties then found a significant correlation between measures of black freedom from economic coercion and black political mobilization. This further corroborated the hypothesis that economic coercion depressed black political mobilization in the Mississippi black belt and suggested that such coercion might explain low levels of black mobilization across the rural Deep South.

The results of this study are summarized in Lester M. Salamon and Stephen Van Evera, "Fear, Apathy, and Discrimination: A Test of Three Explanations of Political Participation," *American Political Science Review* 67 (December, 1973): 1288–1306. (Unfortunately, our article omits my Holmes county interview and process-tracing data. Still wet behind the ears, I assumed that only large-n tests were valid and never thought to present Holmes county as a case study.)

26. The method of difference is more efficient when the characteristics of available cases are quite homogeneous (that is, when most aspects of most cases are

study variable (SV) and explore them for phenomena associated with it. If values on the study variable are very high (if the SV phenomenon is present in abundance), its causes and effects should also be present in unusual abundance, standing out against the case background. If values on the SV are very low (if the SV phenomenon is nearly absent), its causes and effects should also be conspicuous by their absence.

4. We can select cases with extreme within-case variance in the value on the study variable and explore them for phenomena that covary with it. If values on the study variable vary sharply, its causes and effects should also vary sharply, standing out against the more static case background.

5. Counterfactual analysis can aid inductive theorizing. The analyst examines history, trying to "predict" how events would have unfolded had a few elements of the story been changed, with a focus on varying conditions that seem important and/or manipulable. For instance, to explore the effects of military factors on the likelihood of war, one might ask: "How would pre-1914 diplomacy have evolved if the leaders of Europe had not believed that conquest was easy?" Or, to explore the importance of broad social and political factors in causing Nazi aggression: "How might the 1930s have unfolded had Hitler died in 1932?" The greater the impact of the posited changes, the more important the analysis.

When analysts discover counterfactual analyses they find persuasive, they have found theories they find persuasive, since all counterfactual predictions rest on theories. (Without theories the analyst could not predict how changed conditions would have changed events.) If others doubt the analysis (but cannot expose fatal flaws in it), all the better: the theory may be new, hence a real discovery. At this point the analyst has only to frame the theory in

---

similar). The method of agreement is preferred when the characteristics of cases are heterogeneous (that is, when most aspects of most cases are different).

a general manner so that predictions can be inferred from it and tested. The analyst should ask: "What general causal laws are the dynamics I assert examples of?" The answer is a theory.

Counterfactual analysis helps us recognize theories, not make them. Theories uncovered by counterfactual analysis must exist in the theorist's subconscious before the analysis; otherwise the theorist could not construct the counterfactual scenario. Most people believe in more theories than they know. The hard part is to bring these theories to the surface and express them in general terms. Counterfactual analysis aids this process.

6. Theories can often be inferred from policy debates. Proponents of given policies frame specific cause-effect statements ("If communism triumphs in Vietnam, it will triumph in Thailand, Malaysia, and elsewhere") that can be framed as general theories ("Communist victories are contagious: communist victory in one state raises the odds on communist victory in others"; or, more generally, "Revolution is contagious; revolution in one state raises the odds on revolution in others"). We can test these general theories. Such tests can in turn help resolve the policy debate. Theories inferred in this fashion are sure to have policy relevance, and they merit close attention for this reason.

7. The insights of actors or observers who experienced the event one seeks to explain can be mined for hypotheses. Those who experience a case often observe important unrecorded data that is unavailable to later investigators. Hence they can suggest hypotheses that we could not infer from direct observation alone.[27]

27. I used this technique—the "Delphi method"—to infer a hypothesis explaining why black political mobilization remained low in the rural Deep South even after the passage of the 1965 Voting Rights Act. At that time (1969) political scientists widely assumed that low black political mobilization stemmed from black political apathy. I thought the skill of local organizers might be key. Interviews, however, revealed that rural black community leaders doubted both theories. They instead argued that fear of white coercion deterred black participation, and freedom from coercion helped explain pockets of black political mobiliza-

8. Large-n data sets can be explored for correlations between variables. We nominate discovered correlations as possible cause-effect relationships. This method is seldom fruitful, however. A new large-n data set is usually hard to assemble, but if we rely on existing data sets, our purview is narrowed by the curiosities of previous researchers. We can only explore theories that use variables that others have already chosen to code.

9. We can fashion theories by importing existing theories from one domain and adapting them to explain phenomena in another.[28] Thus students of misperception in international relations and students of mass political behavior have both borrowed theories from psychology. Students of military affairs have borrowed theories from the study of organizations. Students of international systems have borrowed theories (e.g., oligopoly theory) from economics.

How Can Theories Be Tested?

We have two basic ways to test theories: experimentation and observation. Observational tests come in two varieties: large-n and case study. Thus, overall we have a universe of three basic testing methods: experimentation, observation using large-n analysis, and observation using case-study analysis.[29]

---

tion. Further investigation found substantial evidence to support their argument. (This hypothesis also emerged from a method-of-difference comparison of two Mississippi counties. See note 25.)

28. Suggesting this technique is Shively, *Craft of Political Research*, p. 165.

29. Deduction supplies a fourth way to evaluate theories. Using deduction to evaluate the hypothesis that a causes b, we would ask if a and b are examples of more general phenomena (A and B) that are already known to cause each other. If so, we can deduce that, since A causes B, and a and b are examples of A and B, then a must cause b. On deductive assessment of theory see, e.g., Hempel's discussion of "theoretical support" for theories in his *Philosophy of Natural Science*, pp. 38–40, and his related discussion of "deductive-nomological" explanations and "covering laws" on page 51 of the same work. The former are explana-

1. *Experimentation.* An investigator infers predictions from a theory. Then the investigator exposes only one of two equivalent groups to a stimulus. Are results congruent or incongruent with the predictions? Congruence of prediction and result corroborates the theory, incongruence infirms it.

2. *Observation.* An investigator infers predictions from a theory. Then the investigator passively observes the data without imposing an external stimulus on the situation and asks if observations are congruent with predictions.[30]

Predictions frame observations we expect to make if our theory is valid. They define expectations about the incidence, sequence, location, and structure of phenomena.[31] For instance, we can always predict that values on the independent and dependent variables of valid theories should covary across time and space, other things being equal. Values on intervening variables that form the theory's explanation should also covary with the independent variable across time and space. Variance on the independent vari-

---

tions that operate by deduction from general laws, the latter are general laws from which specific explanations are deduced.

Most "commonsense" explanations are theories we accept because they are supported by deductions of this sort; however, a deductive evaluation is not a test of a theory. Rather, it applies a previously tested law to a new situation.

30. Observation research designs are also called "quasi-experimental." See Donald T. Campbell and Julian C. Stanley, *Experimental and Quasi-Experimental Designs for Research* (Boston: Houghton Mifflin, 1963), p. 34.

31. I use "prediction" to define expectations about the occurrence of phenomena in both the past and the future if a theory is valid. Others call these expectations the "observable implications" or the "test implications" of theory. King, Keohane, and Verba, *Designing Social Inquiry,* pp. 28–29 and passim; Hempel, *Philosophy of Natural Science,* pp. 7, 30. Still others use "postdiction" to refer to expectations about what the historical record will reveal, reserving "prediction" for expectations about the future.

We use predictions to design tests for hypotheses, but predictions are also hypotheses themselves. They frame phenomena that the independent variable should cause if the hypothesis operates. These phenomena include observable aspects of the dependent variable or intervening variables and effects that these variables produce. Thus the distinction between a prediction and a hypothesis lies not in their nature but the use to which they are put.

able should precede in time related variance on the dependent variable. If a social theory is being tested, actors should speak and act in a manner fitting the theory's logic (for example, if "commercial competition causes war," elites deciding for war should voice commercial concerns as reasons for war).

Some hard sciences (chemistry, biology, physics) rely largely on experiments. Others (astronomy, geology, paleontology) rely largely on observation. In political science experiments are seldom feasible, with rare exceptions such as conflict simulations or psychology experiments. This leaves observation as our prime method of testing.

Two types of observational analysis are possible.:

1. *Large-n,* or "statistical," analysis.[32] A large number of cases—usually several dozen or more—is assembled and explored to see if variables covary as the theory predicts.

2. *Case-study* analysis. The analyst explores a small number of cases (as few as one) in detail, to see whether events unfold in the manner predicted and (if the subject involves human behavior) whether actors speak and act as the theory predicts.[33]

Which method—experiment, large-*n,* or case study—is best? We should favor the method that allows the most strong tests. (I discuss strong tests later in this chapter.) More tests are better than fewer; strong tests are better than weak; many strong tests are best, as are methods that allow them. The structure of available data decides which method is strongest for testing a given theory.

---

32. Primers on large-*n* analysis include Babbie, *Practice of Social Research;* Shively, *Craft of Political Research;* William G. Cochran, *Planning and Analysis of Observational Studies* (New York: Wiley, 1983); Edward S. Balian, *How to Design, Analyze, and Write Doctoral or Masters Research,* 2d ed. (Lanham, Md.: University Press of America, 1988); Edward R. Tufte, *Data Analysis for Politics and Policy* (Englewood Cliffs, N.J.: Prentice-Hall, 1974); D. G. Rees, *Essential Statistics;* George W. Snedecor and William G. Cochran, *Statistical Methods* (Ames: Iowa State University Press, 1989); and David Freedman et al., *Statistics,* 2d ed. (New York: Norton, 1991).

33. Landmark writings on the case-study method are listed in note 1 to Chapter 2.

Most theories of war are best tested by case-study methods because the international historical record of prewar politics and diplomacy, which serves as our data, usually lends itself better to deep study of a few cases than to exploration of many cases. A few cases are recorded in great depth (the two World Wars) but the historical record deteriorates sharply as we move beyond the fifteenth or twentieth case. As a result case studies often allow more and stronger tests than large-n methods. Conversely, large-n methods are relatively more effective for testing theories of American electoral politics because very large numbers of cases (of elections, or of interviewed voters) are well recorded. Case studies can be strong tools for exploring American politics, however, especially if in-depth case studies yield important data that is otherwise inaccessible,[34] and large-n analysis can be a strong method for exploring international politics if relevant test data is recorded for many cases (see, for example, the many good large-n tests of democratic peace theory.)[35] Experimentation is the least valuable approach because experiments are seldom feasible in political science.

Strong vs. Weak Tests; Predictions and Tests

Strong tests are preferred because they convey more information and carry more weight than weak tests.[36]

34. Examples include Richard E. Fenno, *Home Style: House Members in Their Districts* (New York: HarperCollins, 1978), and Fiorina, *Congress: Keystone of the Washington Establishment.*
35. For example, Steve Chan, "Mirror, Mirror on the Wall . . . Are the Freer Countries More Pacific?" *Journal of Conflict Resolution* 28 (December 1984): 617–48; Erich Weede, "Democracy and War Involvement," ibid., pp. 649–64; and Zeev Maoz and Bruce Russett, "Normative and Structural Causes of Democratic Peace, 1946–1986," *American Political Science Review* 87 (September 1993): 624–38.
36. Discussions of strong tests include Eckstein, "Case Study and Theory," pp. 113–31, discussing what he terms "crucial-case studies" (his term for cases supplying strong tests), and Arthur L. Stinchcombe, *Constructing Social Theories* (New York: Harcourt, Brace & World, 1968), pp. 20–22.

A strong test is one whose outcome is unlikely to result from any factor except the operation or failure of the theory. Strong tests evaluate predictions that are *certain* and *unique*. A *certain* prediction is an unequivocal forecast. The more certain the prediction, the stronger the test. The most certain predictions are deterministic forecasts of outcomes that must inexorably occur if the theory is valid. If the prediction fails, the theory fails, since failure can arise only from the theory's nonoperation. A *unique* prediction is a forecast not made by other known theories. The more unique the prediction, the stronger the test. The most unique predictions forecast outcomes that could have no plausible cause except the theory's action. If the prediction succeeds, the theory is strongly corroborated because other explanations for the test outcome are few and implausible.

Certainty and uniqueness are both matters of degree. Predictions fall anywhere on a scale from zero to perfect on both dimensions. Tests of predictions that are highly certain and highly unique are strongest, since they provide decisive positive and negative evidence. As the degree of certitude or uniqueness falls, the strength of the test also falls. Tests of predictions that have little certitude or uniqueness are weakest, and are worthless if the tested prediction has no certitude or uniqueness.

We can distinguish four types of tests, differing by their combinations of strength and weakness:

1. *Hoop tests*. Predictions of high certitude and no uniqueness provide decisive negative tests: a flunked test kills a theory or explanation, but a passed test gives it little support. For example: "Was the accused in the state on the day of the murder?" If not, he is innocent, but showing that he was in town does not prove him guilty. To remain viable the theory must jump through the hoop this test presents, but passage of the test still leaves the theory in limbo.

2. *Smoking-gun tests*. Predictions of high uniqueness and no certitude provide decisive positive tests: passage strongly corrobo-

rates the explanation, but a flunk infirms it very little. For example, a smoking gun seen in a suspect's hand moments after a shooting is quite conclusive proof of guilt, but a suspect not seen with a smoking gun is not proven innocent. An explanation passing a "smoking-gun" test of this sort is strongly corroborated, but little doubt is cast on an explanation that fails it.

3. *Doubly-decisive tests.* Predictions of high uniqueness and high certitude provide tests that are decisive both ways: passage strongly corroborates an explanation, a flunk kills it. If a bank security camera records the faces of bank robbers, its film is decisive both ways—it proves suspects guilty or innocent. Such a test combines a "hoop test" and "smoking-gun" test in a single study. Such tests convey the most information (one test settles the matter) but are rare.

4. *Straw-in-the-wind tests.* Most predictions have low uniqueness and low certitude, and hence provide tests that are indecisive both ways: passed and flunked tests are both "straws in the wind." Such test results can weigh in the total balance of evidence but are themselves indecisive. Thus many explanations for historical events make probabilistic predictions ("If Hitler ordered the Holocaust, we should probably find some written record of his orders")[37], whose failure may simply reflect the downside probabilities. We learn something by testing such straw-in-the-wind predictions, but such tests are never decisive by themselves.[38] Unfortunately, this describes the predictions we usually work with.

Interpretive disputes often arise from disputes over what outcomes theories predict. Does Realism make predictions that were

37. In fact there is no written record of an order from Hitler mandating the Holocaust, yet historians agree that Hitler did order it. A discussion is Sebastian Haffner, *The Meaning of Hitler,* trans. Ewald Osers (Cambridge: Harvard University Press, 1979), pp. 133, 138–43.

38. These last four terms—"hoop test," "smoking-gun test," "doubly-decisive test," and "straw-in-the-wind test"—are my effort to fill gaps in the lexicon.

contradicted by the end of the cold war? Some scholars say yes, others say no. Such disagreements can be narrowed if theories are clearly framed to begin with (since vague theoretical statements leave more room for divergent predictions) and if tested predictions are explained and justified.

Interpretive disputes also arise from quarrels over the uniqueness and certitude of predictions. Is the prediction unique? That is, do other theories or explanations predict the same result? If so, a passed test is less impressive. The Fischer school of historians argues that the December 8, 1912, German "war council," a sinister meeting between Kaiser Wilhelm II and his military leaders (uncovered only in the 1960s), signaled a plot among the German elite to instigate a major war.[39] Some critics answer that the Kaiser's mercurial personality explains his bellicose talk at that meeting—he often blew off steam by saying things he did not mean. In short, they point to a competing explanation for events that some Fischerites claimed was a "smoking gun" for their elite-plot theory of the war. The question then rides on the plausibility of this competing explanation.

Is the prediction certain, in other words, is it unequivocal? If not, flunked tests are less damaging. Some historians argue that the Spanish-American war of 1898 arose from a conspiracy of empire-seeking U.S. leaders who hoped to seize the Philippines from Spain. The absence of any mention of such a conspiracy in these leaders' diaries and private letters or in official archives convinces others that there was none. In this view the conspiracy theory predicts with high certainty that mention of a conspiracy should be found in these records. Conspiracy theorists answer

---

39. On the "war council" see Imanuel Geiss, *German Foreign Policy, 1871–1914* (Boston: Routledge & Kegan Paul, 1976), pp. 142–45, 206–7. Good friendly surveys of the Fischer school's arguments are ibid., and John A. Moses, *The Politics of Illusion: The Fischer Controversy in German Historiography* (London: George Prior, 1975). More critical is John W. Langdon, *July 1914: The Long Debate, 1918–1990* (New York: Berg, 1990), pp. 66–129.

that good conspirators hide their conspiracies, often leaving no records. The conspiracy theory is still alive, they argue, because the theory predicts only weakly that conspirators should record their conspiracy, hence the lack of such a record is a mere "straw in the wind" that infirms the theory only weakly. The question hinges not on the evidence but on divergent estimates of the certitude of the theory's prediction that a conspiracy would leave a visible record.

This discussion highlights the need to discuss the uniqueness and certitude of tested predictions when interpreting evidence. All evidence is not equal because the predictions they test are not equally unique or certain. Hence authors should comment on the uniqueness and certitude of their predictions.

Strong tests are preferred to weak tests, but tests can also be hyper-strong, or unfair to the theory. For example, one can perform tests under conditions where countervailing forces are present that counteract its predicted action. Passage of such tests is impressive because it shows the theory's cause has large importance, that is, high impact. But a valid theory may flunk such tests because a countervailing factor masks its action. Such a test misleads by recording a false negative—unless the investigator, mindful of the test's bias, gives the theory bonus points for the extra hardship it faces.

Another form of hyper-strong test evaluates theories under circumstances that lack the antecedent conditions they require to operate. Again the theory is unlikely to pass, and we are impressed if it does. Passage suggests that the theory has wider explanatory range than previously believed. Such tests are not fair measures of a theory's basic validity, however, since they assess it against claims that it does not make.[40]

40. Advocates of testing theories against "least-likely" cases—cases that ought to invalidate theories if any cases can be expected to do so—recommend a hyper-strong test of this sort if the case they recommend is least-likely because it lacks conditions needed for the theory to operate. A flunked test then tells us that the

Helpful Hints for Testing Theories

Theory-testers should follow these injunctions:
1. Test as many of a theory's hypotheses as possible. Testing only a subset of a theory's hypotheses is bad practice because it leaves the theory partly tested. A theory is fully tested by testing all its parts.
The number of testable hypotheses exceeds the number of links in a theory. Consider the theory:

$$A \rightarrow q \rightarrow r \rightarrow B$$

A complete test would evaluate the theory's prime hypothesis ($A \rightarrow B$), the theory's explanatory hypotheses ($A \rightarrow q$, $q \rightarrow r$, and $r \rightarrow B$), and their hybrid combinations ($A \rightarrow r$ and $q \rightarrow B$). Thus a three-link theory comprises a total of six testable hypotheses. An analyst should explore them all, if time and energy permit.
2. Infer and test as many predictions of each hypothesis as possible. Most hypotheses make several testable predictions, so don't be quickly content to rest with one. To find more, consider what variance the hypothesis predicts across both time and space (that is, across regions, groups, institutions, or individuals). Consider also what decision process (if any) it predicts, and what specific individual speech and action it predicts.
Predictions frame observations you expect to make if the theory is valid. They define expectations about the incidence, sequence, location, and structure of phenomena. Avoid framing tautological predictions that forecast simply that we expect to observe the theory in operation ("If the theory is valid, I predict we will observe its cause causing its effect"). Thus the hypothesis that

---

theory will not operate if its antecedent conditions are absent, but it tells us nothing about the theory's validity when these conditions are met. Such tests are useful and appropriate if the scope of a theory's application is the main question, but are inappropriate if the validity of the theory is the question at issue. Discussing least-likely cases is Eckstein, "Case Study and Theory," p. 118.

"democracy causes peace" yields the following tautological prediction: "We should observe democracy causing peace." A non-
tautological prediction would be: "We should observe that
democratic states are involved in fewer wars than authoritarian
states."

3. Explain and defend the predictions you infer from your theory. As I noted earlier, scientific controversies often stem from
disputes over which predictions can be fairly inferred from a theory and which cannot be. We then see scientists agree on the data
but differ over their interpretation because they disagree on what
the tested theories predict. Theorists can minimize such disputes
by fully explaining and defending their predictions.

Predictions can be either general (the theorist predicts a broad
pattern) or specific (the theorist predicts discrete facts or other
single observations). General predictions are inferred from, and
are used to test, general hypotheses ("If windows of opportunity
and vulnerability drive states to war, states in relative decline
should launch more than their share of wars"). Specific predictions are inferred from, and are used to test, both general hypotheses ("If windows of opportunity and vulnerability drive states to
war, we should see Japan behave more aggressively as a window
of opportunity opened in its favor in 1941") and specific explanations ("If a window of opportunity drove Japan to war in 1941 we
should find records of Japanese decision makers citing a closing
window as reason for war").

4. Select data that represent, as accurately as possible, the domain of the test. When using large-n test methods, select data that
represent the universe defined by tested hypotheses. When using
case-study methods, select data that represent conditions in the
cases studied. Even data that represent the domain of the test only
crudely can be useful.[41] Still, the more accurate the representation,

---

41. John J. Mearsheimer, "Assessing the Conventional Balance: The 3:1 Rule and
Its Critics," *International Security* 13 (Spring 1989): 56–62, argues for and illus-

the better. Choosing evidence selectively—that is, favoring evidence that supports your hypothesis over disconfirming counterevidence—is disallowed, since such a practice violates the principle of accurate representation.

This rule is almost a platitude, but older political science literature (I am thinking of works in international relations) often broke it by "arguing by example." Examples are useful to illustrate deductive theories but only become evidence if they represent (even crudely) the complete relevant data base, and/or they are presented in enough detail to comprise a single case study.

5. Consider and evaluate the possibility that an observed relationship between two variables is not causal but rather results from the effect of a third variable.[42] Two variables may covary because one causes the other, or because a third variable causes both. For example, monthly sales of mittens and snow blowers correlate closely in the northern United States, but neither causes the other. Instead, winter weather causes both. We should consider or introduce controls on the effects of such third variables before concluding that correlation between variables indicates causation between them.

6. When interpreting results, judge each theory on its own merits.

If you flunk (or pass) a theory, do not assume a priori that the same verdict applies to similar theories. Each theory in a theory family (such as the neoclassical family of economic theories, the Marxist family of theories of imperialism, the Realist family of theories of international relations, and so on) should be judged on its own. The strengths and weaknesses of other theories in the family should not be ascribed to it unless both theories are vari-

---

trates the utility of "rule of thumb" tests using data that not selected for its representativeness.
42. A discussion is Babbie, *Practice of Social Research*, pp. 396–409.

ants of the same more general theory and your test has refuted or corroborated that general theory.

If you flunk (or pass) one hypothesis in a multihypothesis theory, this says nothing about the validity of other hypotheses in the theory. Some may be false and others true. You should test each separately.

Consider whether you can repair flunked theories before discarding them. Flunked theories often contain valid hypotheses. Perhaps they can be salvaged and incorporated into a new theory.

7. We can repair theories by replacing disconfirmed hypotheses with new explanatory hypotheses proposing a different intervening causal process or by narrowing the scope of the theory's claims. We narrow a theory's claims by adding new antecedent conditions (condition variables, or CVs), so the theory no longer claims to govern the cases comprised in the flunked test. This allows us to set aside the flunked test. The theory is now more modest but passes its tests.

8. We can test theories against the null hypothesis (the test asks, "Does this theory have *any* explanatory power?") or against each other (the tests asks, "Does this theory have *more* or *less* explanatory power than competing theories?").[43] Both test formats are useful but should not be confused. Theories that pass all their tests against the null should not be named the leading theory without

---

43. Imre Lakatos likewise distinguishes "a two-cornered fight between theory and experiment" and "three-cornered fights between rival theories and experiment." His "two-cornered fights" are tests against the null hypothesis (the hypothesis of no causal relationship); his "three-cornered fights" include a test against the null and a theory-against-theory test. Imre Lakatos, "Falsification and the Methodology of Scientific Research Programmes," in Imre Lakatos and Alan Musgrave, eds., *Criticism and the Growth of Knowledge* (Cambridge: Cambridge University Press, 1970), p. 115. Works formatted as two-cornered fights include many studies on democratic peace theory, for instance, Chan, "Mirror, Mirror on the Wall," and Weede, "Democracy and War Involvement." A study formatted as a three-cornered fight is Barry R. Posen, *The Sources of Military Doctrine: Britain, France, and Germany Between the World Wars* (Ithaca, N.Y.: Cornell University Press, 1984). For more on the topic see Hempel's discussion of "crucial tests" in his *Philosophy of Natural Science*, pp. 25–28.

further investigation; they can still lose contests against competing theories. Conversely, theories that lose contests against competitors should not be dismissed altogether. They may still have some explanatory power, and theories with explanatory power are valuable even if other theories have more.

9. One tests a theory by asking if the empirical evidence confirms the theory's predictions, not by asking how many cases the theory can explain. A theory may explain few cases because its causal phenomenon is rare or because it requires special hothouse conditions to operate, but can still operate strongly when these conditions are present. Such a theory explains few cases but is nevertheless valid.

The number of cases a theory explains does shed light on its utility: the more cases the theory explains, the more useful the theory, other things being equal. Still, even theories that explain very few cases are valuable if these cases are important and the theory explains them well.

10. One does not test a theory by assessing the validity of its assumptions (the assumed values on its CVs). A test asks: "Does the theory operate if the conditions that it claims to require for its operation are present?" Framed this way, a test axiomatically assumes assumptions are true. Tests under conditions that violate the theory's assumptions are unfair, and theories should not be rejected because they flunk such tests.

The validity of a theory's assumptions does affect its utility, however. Assumptions that never hold give rise to theories that operate only in an imaginary world and thus cannot explain reality or generate policy prescriptions.[44] The most useful theories are

---

44. For a different view see Friedman, *Essays in Positive Economics*, pp. 14–23: "In general, the more significant the theory, the more unrealistic the assumptions" (p. 14). Friedman's claim stems from his exclusive focus on the ability of theories to accurately predict outcomes (the values of dependent variables). He is uninterested in the validity of the inner workings of theories, including their explanations as well as their assumptions. This unconcern is appropriate if knowledge

those whose assumptions match reality in at least some important cases.

How Can Specific Events Be Explained?

Ideas framing cause and effect come in two broad types: theories and specific explanations. Theories are cast in general terms and could apply to more than one case ("Expansionism causes war," or "Impacts by extraterrestrial objects cause mass extinctions"). Specific explanations explain discrete events—particular wars, interventions, empires, revolutions, or other single occurrences ("German expansionism caused World War II," or "An asteroid impact caused the extinction of the dinosaurs"). I have covered the framing and testing of theories above, but how should we evaluate specific explanations?[45] We should ask four questions:

1. Does the explanation exemplify a valid general theory (that is to say, a covering law)?[46] To assess the hypothesis that A caused b in a specific instance, we first assess the general form of the hypothesis ("A causes B"). If A does not cause B, we can rule out all explanations of specific instances of B that assert that examples of A were the cause, including the hypothesis that A caused b in this case.

---

about the nature of the theory's inner workings is not useful, but this is seldom the case in the study of politics.

45. The role of theories in historical explanation has long been debated by historians and philosophers of social science. My remarks here follow Hempel, "Function of General Laws in History," the landmark work in the debate. For criticisms and other reactions see Martin and McIntyre, *Readings in the Philosophy of Social Science,* pp. 55–156. A recent discussion is Clayton Roberts, *The Logic of Historical Explanation* (University Park: Pennsylvania State University Press, 1996). See also Eckstein, "Case Study and Theory," pp. 99–104, who discusses "disciplined-configurative" case studies, that is, case studies that aim to explain the case by use of general theories.

46. A general theory from which a specific explanation is deduced is the "covering law" for the explanation. See Hempel, *Philosophy of Natural Science,* p. 51.

We assess the argument that "the rooster's crows caused today's sunrise" by asking whether, in general, roosters cause sunrises by their crowing. If the hypothesis that "rooster crows cause sunrises" has been tested and flunked, we can infer that the rooster's crow cannot explain today's sunrise. The explanation fails because the covering law is false.

Generalized specific explanations are preferred to nongeneralized specific explanations because we can measure the conformity of the former but not the latter to their covering laws. (The latter leave us with no identified covering laws to evaluate.) Nongeneralized specific explanations must be recast as generalized specific explanations before we can measure this conformity.

2. Is the covering law's causal phenomenon present in the case we seek to explain? A specific explanation is plausible only if the value on the independent variable of the general theory on which the explanation rests is greater than zero. Even if A is a confirmed cause of B, it cannot explain instances of B that occur when A is absent.

Even if economic depressions cause war, they cannot explain wars that occur in periods of prosperity. Even if capitalism causes imperialism it cannot explain communist or precapitalist empires. Asteroid impacts may cause extinctions, but cannot explain extinctions that occurred in the absence of an impact.

3. Are the covering law's antecedent conditions met in the case? Theories cannot explain outcomes in cases that omit their necessary antecedent conditions. Dog bites spread rabies if the dog is rabid; bites by a nonrabid dog cannot explain a rabies case.

4. Are the covering law's intervening phenomena observed in the case? Phenomena that link the covering law's posited cause and effect should be evident and appear in appropriate times and places. Thus if an asteroid impact killed the dinosaurs 65 million years ago, we should find evidence of the catastrophic killing process that an impact would unleash. For example, some scien-

tists theorize that an impact would kill by spraying the globe with molten rock, triggering forest fires that would darken the skies with smoke, shut out sunlight, and freeze the earth. If so, we should find the soot from these fires in 65-million-year-old sediment worldwide. We should also find evidence of a very large (continent-sized or even global) molten rock shower and a very abrupt dying of species.[47]

This fourth step is necessary because the first three steps are not definitive. If we omit step 4, it remains possible that the covering law that supports our explanation is probabilistic and the case at hand is among those where it did not operate.[48] We also should test the explanation's within-case predictions as a hedge against the possibility that our faith in the covering law is misplaced, and that the "law" is in fact false. For these two reasons, the better the details of the case conform to the detailed within-case predictions of the explanation, the stronger the inference that the explanation explains the case.[49]

---

47. In fact the sedimentary record laid down at the time of the dinosaurs' demise confirms these predictions. Walter Alvarez and Frank Asaro, "An Extraterrestrial Impact," *Scientific American*, October 1990, pp. 79–82.

The debate over the dinosaur extinction nicely illustrates the inference and framing of clear predictions from specific explanations. On the impact theory see Alvarez and Asaro, "Extraterrestrial Impact"; Vincent Courtillot, "A Volcanic Eruption," *Scientific American*, October 1990, pp. 85–92; and William J. Broad, "New Theory Would Reconcile Views on Dinosaurs' Demise," *New York Times*, December 27, 1994, p. C1.

48. The cause of probabilism in probabilistic causal laws usually lies in variance in the values of antecedent conditions that we have not yet identified. By identifying these conditions and including them in our theory we make its law less probabilistic and more deterministic.

49. Less convinced of the need for this last step is Hempel, "Function of General Laws in History," who rests with the first three steps and omits the fourth. Hempel assumes that his covering laws are deterministic (not probabilistic) and are well proven. Most social science laws are probabilistic, however, and most are poorly established. Hence deducing the validity of a specific explanation from the first three steps alone is unreliable, and we should also seek empirical verification that the explanation's causal process in fact occurred before reaching final conclusions.

Analysts are allowed to infer the covering law that underlies the specific explanation of a given event from the event itself. The details of the event suggest a specific explanation; the analyst then frames that explanation in general terms that allow tests against a broader database; the explanation passes these tests; and the analyst then reapplies the theory to the specific case. Thus the testing of the general theory and the explaining of a specific case can be done together and can support each other.

Methodology Myths

Philosophers of social science offer many specious injunctions that can best be ignored. The following are among them:

1. "Evidence infirming theories transcends in importance evidence confirming theories." Karl Popper and other falsificationists argue that "theories are not verifiable," only falsifiable,[50] and that tests infirming a theory are far more significant than tests confirming it.[51] Their first claim is narrowly correct, their second is not. Theories cannot be proved absolutely because we cannot imagine and test every prediction they make, and the possibility always remains that an unimagined prediction will fail. By contrast, infirming tests can more decisively refute a theory. It does not follow that infirming tests transcend confirming tests, however. If a theory passes many strong tests but then flunks a test of a previously untested prediction, this usually means that the theory requires previously unidentified antecedent conditions to operate.

50. Karl R. Popper, *The Logic of Scientific Discovery* (London: Routledge, 1995), p. 252. A criticism of Popper and falsificationism is King, Keohane, and Verba, *Constructing Social Inquiry*, pp. 100–103.
51. In a friendly summary of falsificationism David Miller writes that to falsificationists "the passing of tests . . . makes not a jot of difference to the status of any hypothesis, though the failing of just one test may make a great deal of difference." David Miller, "Conjectural Knowledge: Popper's Solution of the Problem of Induction," in Paul Levinson, ed., *In Pursuit of Truth* (Atlantic Highlands, N.J.: Humanities Press, 1988), p. 22.

We react by reframing the theory to include the antecedent condition, thus narrowing the scope of the theory's claims to exclude the flunked test. In Popper's terms we now have a new theory; however, all the tests passed by the old theory also corroborate the new, leaving it in very strong shape at birth. Thus confirming tests tell us a great deal—about the old theory, about its repaired replacement, and about any later versions. Popper's contrary argument stems partly from his strange assumption that once theories are stated they are promptly accepted,[52] hence evidence in their favor is unimportant because it merely reinforces a preexisting belief in the theory. The opposite is more often true: most new ideas face hostile prejudice even after confirming evidence accumulates.[53]

2. "Theories cannot be falsified before their replacement emerges." Imre Lakatos claims that "there is no falsification [of theory] before the emergence of a better theory," and "falsification cannot precede the better theory."[54] This claim is too sweeping. It applies only to theories that fail some tests but retain some explanatory power. We should retain these theories until a stronger replacement arrives. But if testing shows that a theory has no explanatory power, we should reject it whether or not a replacement theory is at hand.[55] Many science programs—for example, medical research—advance by routinely testing theories against null hypotheses and rejecting those that fail, whether or not replacements are ready.

52. See King, Keohane, and Verba, *Designing Social Inquiry,* p. 100.
53. A famous development of this argument is Thomas S. Kuhn, *The Structure of Scientific Revolutions,* 2d enlarged edition (Chicago: University of Chicago Press, 1970).
54. Lakatos, "Falsification and the Methodology of Scientific Research Programmes," pp. 119, 122.
55. An early reader of this chapter suggested that Lakatos meant only that falsification of theories that retain some explanatory power cannot precede the better theory, following the argument I suggest here. That may be the case. Lakatos's arguments are well hidden in tortured prose that gives new meaning to the phrase "badly written," and no reading of such dreadful writing is ever certain or final.

Asking those who claim to refute theories or explanations to propose plausible replacements can serve as a check on premature claims of refutation. This can expose instances where the refuting investigator held the theory to a standard that their own explanation could not meet. This suggests in turn that the standard was too high, in other words, that the refuter misconstrued noise in the data as decisive falsifying evidence against the theory. However, finding merit in this exercise is a far cry from agreeing that theories cannot be falsified except by the greater success of competing theories. Surely we can know what is wrong before knowing what is right.

3. "The evidence that inspired a theory should not be reused to test it." This argument[56] is often attached to warnings not to test theories with the same cases from which they were inferred. It rests on a preference for blind testing.[57] The assumption is that data not used to infer a theory is less well known to an investigator than used data, hence the investigator using unused data is less tempted to sample the data selectively.

Blind testing is a useful check on dishonesty, but is not viable as a fixed rule. Its purpose is to prevent scholars from choosing corroborating tests while omitting infirming ones. But imposing blind-test rules on social science is in fact impossible because investigators nearly always know something about their data before they test their theories and thus often have a good idea what tests will show even if they exclude the data that inspired their ideas.

56. Raising this issue are Alexander L. George and Timothy J. McKeown, "Case Studies and Theories of Organizational Decision Making," in *Advances in Information Processing in Organizations* (Greenwich, Conn.: JAI Press, 1985), 2:38; David Collier, "The Comparative Method," in Ada W. Finifter, ed., *Political Science: The State of the Discipline*, 2d ed. (Washington, D.C.: American Political Science Association, 1993), p. 115; and King, Keohane, and Verba, *Designing Social Inquiry*, pp. 21–23, 46, 141, who note "the problem of using the same data to generate and test a theory . . ." (p. 23) and argue that "we should always try to . . . avoid using the same data to evaluate the theory that we used to develop it" (p. 46).

57. A discussion is Hempel, *Philosophy of Natural Science*, pp. 37–38.

Hence we need other barriers against test fudging.[58] Infusing social science professions with high standards of honesty is the best
solution.

4. "Do not select cases on the dependent variable"—that is, do
not select cases of what you seek to explain (for example, wars)
without also choosing cases of the contrary (peace). Students of
the case method often repeat this warning.[59] It is not valid. Selection on the dependent variable is appropriate under any of three
common conditions:

a. If we can compare conditions in selected cases to a known
average situation.[60] The average situation is often sufficiently well
known not to require further descriptive study. If so, we can com-

---

58. Moreover, a blind-test requirement would generate a preposterous double
standard in the right to use evidence: the same data would be forbidden as test
material to some scholars (because they inferred the theory from it) while being
allowed to others. How would this rule be administered? Who would record
which scholars had used which data for theory-making, and hence were barred
from reusing it for testing? Would we establish a central registry of hypotheses
where theorists would record the origins of their ideas? How would we verify
and penalize failure to accurately record hypotheses with this registry? How
would we deal with the many scholars who are not really sure where their
hypotheses come from?

59. See Barbara Geddes, "How the Cases You Choose Affect the Answers You
Get: Selection Bias in Comparative Cases," *Political Analysis* 2 (1990): 131–50; also
King, Keohane, and Verba, *Designing Social Inquiry*, pp. 108–9, 129–32, 137–38,
140–49. King et al. warn that "we will not learn anything about causal effects"
from studies of cases selected without variation on the dependent variable; they
declare that the need for such variation "seems so obvious that we would think it
hardly needs to be mentioned"; and they conclude that research designs that lack
such variation "are easy to deal with: avoid them!" (pp. 129–30). A criticism is
Ronald Rogowski, "The Role of Scientific Theory and Anomaly in Social-
Scientific Inference," *American Political Science Review* 89 (June 1995): 467–70.
Rogowski notes that King, Keohane, and Verba's strictures point to a "needlessly
inefficient path of social-scientific inquiry," and obedience to these strictures
"may paralyze, rather than stimulate, scientific inquiry" (p. 470). On Geddes and
King, Keohane, and Verba see also David Collier and James Mahoney, "Insights
and Pitfalls: Selection Bias in Qualitative Research," *World Politics* 49 (October
1996): 56–91.

60. Thus Lijphart notes the "implicitly comparative" nature of some single-case
studies. "Comparative Politics and the Comparative Method," pp. 692–93.

pare cases selected on the dependent variable to these known normal conditions. There is no need for full-dress case studies to provide sharper points of comparison.[61]

    b. If the cases have large within-case variance on the study variable, permitting multiple within-case congruence procedures.

    c. If cases are sufficiently data-rich to permit process tracing.[62]

These conditions allow test methods—comparison to average conditions, multiple within-case congruence procedures, and process tracing—that do not require comparison to specific external cases. When they are used, failure to select cases for explicit comparison raises no problems.

    5. "Select for analysis theories that have concepts that are easy to measure." Some scholars recommend we focus on questions that are easy to answer.[63] This criterion is not without logic: study of the fundamentally unknowable is futile and should be avoided. However, the larger danger lies in pointlessly "looking under the light" when the object sought lies in darkness but could with effort be found. Large parts of social science have already diverted their focus from the important to the easily observed, thereby drifting into trivia.[64] Einstein's general theory of relativity proved hard to test. So should he have restrained himself from devising it? The structure of a scientific program is distorted when researchers shy from the logical next question because its answer will be hard to

61. Thus the erring scholars that Geddes identifies erred because they misconstrued the normal worldwide background levels of the key independent variables, e.g. intensity of labor repression, that they studied.

62. On congruence procedure and process tracing see the section "Testing Theories with Case Studies," in Chapter 2.

63. King, Keohane, and Verba warn that "we should choose observable, rather than unobservable, concepts wherever possible. Abstract, unobserved concepts such as utility, culture, intentions, motivations, identification, intelligence, or the national interest are often used in social science theories," but "they can be a hindrance to empirical evaluation of theories . . . unless they can be defined in a way such that they, or at least their implications, can be observed and measured." King, Keohane, and Verba, *Constructing Social Theories*, p. 109.

64. See, for example, the last several decades of the *American Political Science Review*.

find.[65] A better solution is to give bonus credit to scholars who take on the harder task of studying the less observable.

6. "Counterfactual analysis can expand the number of observations available for theory-testing." James Fearon suggests this argument.[66] Counterfactual statements cannot provide a substitute for empirical observations, however. They can clarify an explanation: "I claim x caused y; to clarify my claim, let me explain my image of a world absent x." They can also help analysts surface hypotheses buried in their own minds (see the section "How Can Theories Be Made?" in this chapter). But counterfactual statements are not data and cannot replace empirical data in theory-testing.

65. Moreover, tests that are difficult for the time being may become feasible as new tests are devised or new data emerge. Thus theories of the Kremlin's conduct under Stalin were hard to test before the Soviet collapse but later became more testable. This is another reason to keep hard questions on the agenda.
66. James D. Fearon, "Counterfactuals and Hypothesis Testing in Political Science," *World Politics* 43 (January 1991): 171 and passim.

CHAPTER 2

What Are Case Studies?
How Should They
Be Performed?

A large literature on the case-study method has appeared in
recent years,[1] but that literature remains spotty. No complete
catalog of research designs for case studies has emerged.[2] No
textbook covers the gamut of study design considerations.[3] There

1. A good survey of the case-study literature is David Collier, "The Comparative
Method," in Ada W. Finifter, ed., *Political Science: The State of the Discipline*, 2d ed.
(Washington, D.C.: American Political Science Association, 1993), pp. 105–20.
Landmark writings on the case method include Alexander L. George and Timo-
thy J. McKeown, "Case Studies and Theories of Organizational Decision Mak-
ing," in *Advances in Information Processing in Organizations* (Greenwich, Conn.:
JAI Press, 1985), 2:21–58; Arend Lijphart, "Comparative Politics and the Com-
parative Method," *American Political Science Review* 65 (September 1971): 682–93;
Harry Eckstein, "Case Study and Theory in Political Science," in Fred I. Greenstein and Nelson W. Polsby, ed., *Handbook of Political Science*, vol. 7, *Strategies of
Inquiry* (Reading, Mass.: Addison-Wesley, 1975), pp. 79–137; and Robert K. Yin,
Case Study Research: Design and Methods, 2d ed. (Thousand Oaks, Calif.: Sage,
1994). A more developed discussion by George is Alexander L. George, "Case
Studies and Theory Development" (paper presented to the Second Annual Symposium on Information Processing in Organizations, Carnegie-Mellon University, Pittsburgh, Pa., October 15–16, 1982). An earlier statement is Alexander
George, "Case Studies and Theory Development: The Method of Structured,
Focused Comparison," in Paul Gordon Lauren, ed., *Diplomacy: New Approaches in
History, Theory, and Policy* (New York: Free Press, 1979), pp. 43–68. Additional
works on case methods are listed in the bibliography.
2. Yin, *Case Study Research*, pp. 18–19.
3. Ibid., p. 18. Useful steps toward such a text are Yin's *Case Study Research* and

is no soup-to-nuts cookbook on the case method for beginning practitioners, and many texts on social science methodology slight or omit the case-study method.[4] Accordingly, the following chapter distills, elaborates, and qualifies the observations and suggestions of existing literature. I focus on assessing the case-study method and offering practical how-to-do-it advice for beginners doing case studies.

Case Studies in Perspective

As I noted in Chapter 1, we have two basic ways to test theories: experimentation and observation.[5] Observational tests come in two varieties: large-n and case study. Thus, overall we have a universe of three basic testing methods: experimentation, observation using large-n analysis, and observation using case-study analysis.

Which testing method is best? Is case study inferior to other methods?

Social scientists have long considered case studies the weakest

Gary King, Robert O. Keohane, and Sidney Verba, *Designing Social Inquiry: Scientific Inference in Qualitative Research* (Princeton: Princeton University Press, 1994).
4. Yin, *Case Study Research*, pp. 13, 18–19; Jennifer Platt, "'Case Study' in American Methodological Thought," *Current Sociology* 40 (Spring 1992): 42–43. Works slighting the case-study method include Earl Babbie, *The Practice of Social Research*, 7th ed. (Belmont, Calif.: Wadsworth, 1995); Julian L. Simon and Paul Burstein, *Basic Research Methods in Social Science*, 3d ed. (New York: Random House, 1985); Kenneth D. Bailey, *Methods of Social Research*, 4th ed. (New York: Free Press, 1994); David Dooley, *Social Research Methods*, 3d ed. (Upper Saddle River, N.J.: Prentice-Hall, 1995); and Norman K. Denzin, *The Research Act*, 3d ed. (Englewood Cliffs, N.J.: Prentice-Hall, 1989). Babbie mentions case studies once (p. 280); Simon and Burstein give case-study methods a two-page mention (pp. 37–38); Bailey has three pages that touch the subject (pp. 301–3); Dooley has a chapter on "qualitative research" (pp. 257–74) but no direct mention of case studies.
5. See the section "How Can Theories Be Tested?" in Chapter 1.

of these three testing methods for two reasons.[6] First, some argue that case studies provide the least opportunity to control for the effect of perturbing third variables. In this view experiments are the best method (the investigator eliminates the possible effect of omitted variables by exposing the group to only one stimulus, while holding the others constant). Large-n analysis is next-best, because the investigator can run partial correlations to control the effect of specific omitted variables and can rely on the randomizing effect of examining many cases to reduce the effects of other omitted variables. Studies of one or a few cases are worst, because the data is unrandomized and partial correlations are infeasible, since data points are too few.[7]

This criticism of case studies is unfair, however. Case studies offer two fairly strong methods for controlling the impact of omitted variables. First, tests of predictions of within-case variance

6. See, e.g., Yin, *Case Study Research,* pp. 9–11, who notes the "traditional prejudice against the case study strategy," and the "disdain for the [case-study] strategy" held by many researchers (p. 9). As Yin further notes, texts on social science methodology reflect this disdain by neglecting or omitting the case method: "Most social science textbooks have failed to consider the case method a formal research strategy at all" (p. 13). Randy Stoecker likewise notes the disrepute of case studies among sociologists, who "see the case study as barely better than journalism." Randy Stoecker, "Evaluating and Rethinking the Case Study," *The Sociological Review* 39 (February, 1991): 88. See also Jacques Hamel with Stéphane Dufour and Dominic Fortin, *Case Study Methods* (Newbury Park, Calif.: Sage, 1993), pp. 18–28.
7. Lijphart and Smelser advance this view. See Lijphart, "Comparative Politics and the Comparative Method," pp. 683–84, and Neil J. Smelser, "The Methodology of Comparative Analysis," in Donald P. Warwick and Samuel Osherson, eds., *Comparative Research Methods* (Englewood Cliffs, N.J.: Prentice Hall, 1973), pp. 45, 57. Collier, "Comparative Method," pp. 106–8, summarizes Lijphart. See also Donald T. Campbell and Julian C. Stanley, *Experimental and Quasi-Experimental Designs for Research* (Boston: Houghton Mifflin, 1963), p. 6, who claim that single case studies are "of almost no scientific value." But see further Campbell's later retraction: Donald T. Campbell, "'Degrees of Freedom' and the Case Study," in Donald T. Campbell, *Methodology and Epistemology for Social Science: Selected Papers* (Chicago: University of Chicago Press, 1988, first pub. 1974), pp. 377–88; and noting this retraction, Collier, "Comparative Method," p. 115.

(that is, tests using a multiple "congruence procedure"[8] or a "process-tracing" methodology[9]) gain strong controls from the uniform character of the background conditions of the case.[10] Most cases offer a backdrop of fairly uniform case conditions, and many cases allow a number of observations of values on the independent (IV) and dependent variables (DV). If case conditions are uniform, we can discount third-variable influence as a cause of observed within-case covariance between values on IV and DV. (The uniform background conditions of the case create a semi-controlled environment that limits the effects of third variables by holding them constant.)[11]

Second, we can control the effects of omitted variables by selecting for study cases with extreme (high or low) values on the study variable (SV). This lowers the number of third factors with the strength to produce the result that the test theory predicts,

8. In a multiple-congruence procedure the investigator explores the case looking for congruence or incongruence between observed and predicted values on several or more measures of the independent and dependent variables of the test hypothesis. See the discussion of congruence procedure in the next section of this chapter. To test a theory fully one would look for congruence or incongruence between values of independent and dependent variables, between independent and intervening variables, between intervening variables (if there are several), and between intervening and dependent variables.

9. On "process tracing" see George and McKeown, "Case Studies and Theories," pp. 34–41; George, "Case Studies and Theory Development" (1979), pp. 18–19; and the discussion of process tracing in the next section of this chapter. George and McKeown use "process tracing" to refer to a tracing of "the decision process by which various initial conditions are translated into outcomes." "Case Studies and Theories," p. 35. I use the term more broadly, to refer to the tracing of *any* causal process by which initial conditions are translated into outcomes. Thus my definition includes the tracing of both decision processes and causal processes that do not involve decisions. We might reserve "decision-process tracing" to capture George and McKeown's narrower meaning.

10. Noting the controls that congruence procedure and process tracing allow (and referring to them jointly as "pattern matching") is Campbell, "'Degrees of Freedom' and the Case Study," p. 380.

11. This logic applies to analysis of any hypothesized causal relationship— between IV and IntV, IntV and IntV, or IntV and DV, as well as IV and DV.

which lowers the possibility that omitted variables account for passed tests.[12]

A second criticism of case studies—that "case-study results cannot be generalized to other cases"—has more merit, but applies only to single-case studies. A single case is a poor laboratory for identifying a theory's antecedent conditions (background conditions that activate or magnify its action),[13] because as noted above, most cases provide a backdrop of fairly uniform case conditions. This uniformity masks the action of antecedent conditions that the theory requires, since the antecedent condition does not vary, hence it causes no telltale variance on the DV. Thus a theory that passes a single-case-study test with flying colors may require rare antecedent conditions and hence have little explanatory range,[14] but this weakness can remain hidden from an investigator who studies only one or two cases. (Thus a strength of the case method is also a weakness. The uniformity of case background conditions controls the effects of third variables but also masks antecedent conditions.) The identity and importance of antecedent conditions emerges more clearly from large-n studies. In large-n studies, cases that lack these antecedent conditions emerge as outliers that exhibit the theory's cause without its predicted outcome. The existence of outliers signals that the theory needs

12. On this technique see the discussion of congruence procedure type 1 in the next section of this chapter. A third means of omitted-variable control in case studies is found in the method of controlled comparison, using John Stuart Mill's "method of difference," but this is a fairly weak tool. See the discussion of controlled comparison in the next section of this chapter.
13. The process of defining and measuring the prevalence of the antecedent conditions is often referred to as testing a theory's "external validity," meaning tests "establishing the domain to which a theory can be generalized." Yin, *Case Study Research*, p. 33. Tests for external validity contrast with tests of "internal validity," which address the capacity of the theory to explain a given case. See, for example, Yin, *Case Study Research*, pp. 33, 35–36, and Collier, "Comparative Method," p. 113. I avoid these binary categories because they omit an important third type of validity—the ability of the theory to pass tests in a given case.
14. On explanatory range see the discussion of a theory's explanatory power in the section "What Is a Good Theory?" in Chapter 1.

special conditions to operate; study of these outliers can identify these conditions. The study of a single case offers no parallel method for uncovering antecedent conditions; however, these antecedent conditions can be uncovered by doing more case studies, so this weakness in the case method is reparable.[15]

The case method has two strengths that offset this weakness. First, tests performed with case studies are often strong, because the predictions tested are quite unique (these predictions are not made by other known theories).[16] Specifically, case studies allow the test of predictions about the private speech and writings of policy actors. Often these predictions are singular to the theory that makes them; no other theory predicts the same thoughts or statements. The confirmation of such predictions strongly corroborates the test theory. Case studies are the best format for capturing such evidence. Hence case studies can supply quite decisive evidence for or against political theories. Often this evidence is more decisive than large-n evidence.

Second, inferring and testing explanations that define *how* the independent causes the dependent variable are often easier with case-study than large-n methods. If case-study evidence supports a hypothesis, the investigator can then explore the case further to deduce and test explanations detailing the operation of the hypothesis. Most important, one can "process trace," that is, examine the process whereby initial case conditions are translated into case outcomes. How does the theory work? Tracing process can tell us. Congruence procedures can also illuminate explanations. (More on process tracing and congruence procedures below.) Both procedures are fairly easy to perform after a case has been initially

15. Methods of inferring and testing antecedent conditions with case studies are discussed later in this chapter.
16. As noted in Chapter 1, a test is strong if it evaluates a unique prediction (a forecast not made by other known theories), because the prediction's fulfillment cannot be explained except by the theory's action. Tests are also strong if they evaluate certain predictions (forecasts that are unequivocal and must occur if the theory is valid). On strong and weak tests see the section "Strong vs. Weak Tests" in Chapter 1 and the section "Strong vs. Weak Tests" in this chapter.

studied because the background spadework on the case—establishing the case background and chronology, and so on—has already been done. In contrast, a large-n test of a hypothesis provides little or no new insight into the causal process that comprises the hypothesis' explanation, nor does it generate data that could be used to infer or test explanations of that process. Overall, large-n methods tell us more about whether hypotheses hold than why they hold. Case studies say more about why they hold.

Thus the case method is a strong method of testing theories. Is a theory valid? How does it operate? Even single-case studies can give clear answers. They are less able to identify a theory's antecedent conditions. How broad is the range of cases that the theory governs? Case studies say little unless several are performed.

Which method of inquiry—experiment, large-n, or case study—is superior? The answer turns on the nature of our question and structure of the data in the domain we study. Experiments can be best if experiments are feasible (but they seldom are in social science). Large-n can be best if we want to test a prime hypothesis, and if we have many well-recorded cases to study. Case studies can be best if we want to infer or test explanatory hypotheses, or if cases have been unevenly recorded—a few are recorded in great detail, many in scant detail. There is no uniform answer to the question "which method is best?"

Testing Theories with Case Studies

Case studies can serve five main purposes: testing theories, creating theories, identifying antecedent conditions, testing the importance of these antecedent conditions, and explaining cases of intrinsic importance.[17] The first four purposes are similar in

17. These purposes overlap and several (such as, for example, explaining cases, creating theories and testing theories; and identifying and testing antecedent conditions) often can and should be pursued simultaneously. For another typology of case-study formats see Lijphart, "Comparative Politics and the Compara-

their logic and are realized using the same basic methods. Although each purpose merits its own discussion, readers familiar with this material may wish to skip to the section "Explaining Cases" after reading this one.

Case studies offer three formats for testing theories:[18] controlled comparison, congruence procedures, and process tracing. Controlled comparison uses comparative observations across cases to test theories. Congruence procedures are of two types, with one type using comparative observations across cases to test theories, the other using observations within cases. Process tracing tests theories using observations within cases. Congruence procedure and process tracing are stronger test methods than controlled comparison. (All three are also used to create theories and to infer and test antecedent conditions.)

In each testing format the same three steps should be followed: (1) state the theory; (2) state expectations about what we should observe in the case if the theory is valid, and what we should observe if it is false; and (3) explore the case (or cases) looking for congruence or incongruity between expectation and observation.

Controlled Comparison

In controlled comparison[19] the investigator explores paired observations in two or more cases, asking if values on the pairs are

---

tive Method." He distinguishes six types of case study (p. 691): (1) atheoretical, (2) interpretive, (3) hypothesis-generating, (4) theory confirming, (5) theory infirming, and (6) deviant. Five of Lijphart's categories overlap with three of mine: his study types 4 and 5 are types of theory-testing study, his type 2 is a case-explaining study, and his types 3 and 6 are types of theory-making study. Lijphart's first study-type is descriptive history, a study-type I do not consider here. He omits antecedent-condition-identifying and condition-testing studies, which I consider later in this chapter.

18. Theory-testing case studies are also known as "theory confirming" and "theory infirming" studies. Lijphart, "Comparative Politics and the Comparative Method," p. 692.

19. See George and McKeown, "Case Studies and Theories," pp. 24–29, and works discussed in Collier, "Comparative Method," pp. 111–12 (his section on "Focus on Comparable Cases").

congruent or incongruent with the test theory's predictions. For example, if values on the independent variable (IV) are higher in case *A* than case *B*, values on the dependent variable (DV) should also be higher in case *A* than *B*. If values on the DV are in fact higher in case *A* than *B*, the theory passes the test. If they are much higher, this indicates that the theory has large importance—that variance in the value on the IV will cause large variance in the value on the DV. If they are only a little higher, the test is again passed but the result suggests that the theory has little importance.

Case selection follows John Stuart Mill's "method of difference" or "method of agreement."[20] In the method of difference the investigator chooses cases with similar general characteristics and different values on the study variable (the variable whose causes or effects we seek to establish). If we seek to establish the causes of the study variable, the investigator then asks if values on the study variable correspond across cases with values on variables that define its possible causes. If we seek to establish the effects of the study variable, the investigator asks if its values correspond across cases with values on variables that define its possible effects. In each instance similar cases are picked to control for the effect of third variables: the more similar the cases, the less likely that the action of third variables explains passed tests.

In the method of agreement the investigator chooses cases with different general characteristics and similar values on the study variable. The investigator then asks if values on the study variable correspond across cases with values on variables that define its possible effects (or its causes, if we seek to establish these).

Controlled comparison is the most familiar case-study method but also the weakest. The method of difference is weak because in social science the characteristics of paired cases are never nearly

20. John Stuart Mill, *A System of Logic*, ed. J. M. Robson (Toronto: University of Toronto Press, 1973), chap. 8, "Of the Four Methods of Experimental Inquiry," pp. 388–406. George and McKeown discuss Mill in "Case Studies and Theories," pp. 26–28.

identical (as the method of difference requires). The method of agreement is even weaker because paired cases usually deviate even further from having wholly different characteristics (as the method of agreement requires).[21]

Congruence Procedures

When using congruence procedures[22] the investigator explores the case looking for congruence or incongruence between values observed on the independent and dependent variable and values predicted by the test hypothesis. Two types of congruence procedure are used.

1. *Congruence procedure type 1: Comparison to typical values.* The investigator observes values on the IV and DV within a particular case and observes the world (without doing further case studies) to ascertain values on the IV and DV that are typical in most other cases. The investigator then deduces from these observations and from the test theory expected relative values for the IV and DV in the study case and measures the congruence or incongruence between expectation and observation. For example, in a given case, if the IV's value is above the typical norm, the value on the DV should also be above normal if the theory holds water.[23] If values on the DV are in fact above normal, the theory passes the test. If they are far above normal, this indicates that the theory has large

21. Noting these and other difficulties with controlled comparison are George and McKeown, "Case Studies and Theories," p. 27, and Stanley Lieberson, "Small N's and Big Conclusions: An Examination of the Reasoning in Comparative Studies Based on a Small Number of Cases," *Social Forces* 70 (December 1991): 307–20.

22. On congruence procedure see Alexander L. George, "The Causal Nexus between Cognitive Beliefs and Decision-Making Behavior: The 'Operational Code' Belief System," in Lawrence S. Falkowski, ed., *Psychological Models in International Politics* (Boulder: Westview, 1979), pp. 105–13, and George and McKeown, "Case Studies and Theories," pp. 29–34.

23. If the value on the IV is below normal, the DV's value should also be below normal.

importance, that variance in the value on the IV will cause large variance on the DV. If they are only a little above normal, the test is again passed but the result suggests that the theory has little importance.

Thus to test the hypothesis that "economic downturns cause scapegoating of ethnic minorities," we would explore cases of downturns (for example, the United States in the Great Depression of the 1930s), asking if ethnic scapegoating was above normal in these cases; or we would explore cases of prosperity (the United States in the 1960s) and ask if ethnic scapegoating was below normal.

How do we ascertain normal IV and DV values? Often the normal background levels of phenomena are a matter of common knowledge. Thus we know that the U.S. economy of the 1930s was more depressed than typical modern industrial economies without doing new studies to prove it. We know that Nazi Germany and Stalin's Soviet Union were more murderous than typical modern industrial states, and we can safely compare their conduct to this typical conduct in a case study. We know that elite belief that conquest was feasible was above the historical average in Europe in 1914. If common knowledge is thin or unreliable, however, research to establish typical values is necessary.

Congruence procedure type 1 works best if we select cases with extreme (very high or very low) values on the SV. Thus to test the hypothesis that "economic downturns cause scapegoating of ethnic minorities," we would explore the United States in the 1930s (an extreme downturn) instead of a lesser U.S. or European recession. To test the hypothesis that "belief that conquest is easy causes war," we would explore Europe during 1910–14 (when such beliefs were unusually widespread) instead of more normal times.[24] Cases that exhibit extreme values on study variables are

---

24. An example from physics is found in the test of Einstein's general theory of relativity conducted with photographs of the May 29, 1919, solar eclipse. Eins-

good test laboratories because theories make more unique and certain predictions about them. This allows stronger tests. In a case where a theory's causal phenomenon is extremely abundant its effects (including both its intervening and dependent variables) should also be abundant. Likewise, if the cause is unusually scarce, its effects should also be scarce. If we observe these extreme results, it is unlikely that they arise from measurement error, since only a large error would cause the observed result. The action of a third variable is also an unlikely cause of the observation, since it is unlikely that another cause operates strongly enough to produce the striking effect that the theory predicts. And any third variable that was responsible would also be abundant, hence it would stand out against the case background, making it easy to spot. Hence we can more easily rule out measurement error and omitted-variable explanations for passed tests. (In other words, the tested prediction is quite unique, hence the test is strong.)

If we fail to observe the predicted result, it is less likely that measurement error or the countervailing effect of other variables caused the failure. Since a large result was predicted, that result should have overpowered any measurement errors or countervailing variables, appearing despite them. Moreover, a countervailing variable would probably need to be abundant and hence be easy to spot. Hence a test failure in the absence of a visible powerful countervailing variable casts large doubt on the theory. (In other words, the tested prediction is quite certain, hence the test is strong.)

---

tein's theory predicted that gravity would bend the path of light. Accordingly, scientists looked to the strongest gravity source they could find—the sun—and asked if it could bend the path of light. (Photographs of an eclipse were used because its darkness made stars near the sun visible, letting scientists observe if these stars appeared displaced by its gravity.) In other words, scientists selected a case where the value on the IV (gravity) was as high as possible. On this test see the discussion on process tracing in this section.

Hence both the passage and the flunking of tests provides decisive evidence in cases with extreme values on the study variable. Passage strongly corroborates the hypothesis, a flunk strongly infirms it.

Congruence procedure type 1 is a close cousin of controlled comparison. Both rest on comparisons across cases, not within them.[25] Both offer means to reduce the possibility that passed tests result from the action of third variables. They differ in the method of reducing this possibility. Controlled comparison holds the case background constant, thus preventing the variance of potentially perturbing third variables. Thus it narrows the range of variables that vary across cases, which lowers the number of potential perturbing variables. In contrast, if an "extreme value on study variable" case-selection method is used, congruence type 1 reduces omitted-variable problems by expanding the impact that omitted variables must generate to produce the result predicted by the theory. This lowers the likelihood that any third variables have enough impact to produce this result and also ensures that these variables' necessarily extreme values will call attention to themselves if they do produce this result. Thus the number of potential perturbing variables is again reduced, this time by a different method.

2. *Congruence procedure type 2: Multiple within-case comparisons.* The investigator makes a number of paired observations of values

25. George describes congruence procedure (by which he means Type 1 congruence procedure) as a within-case case study because he argues that congruence or incongruence is established by deduction, not by comparison to typical values in other cases. Specifically, he argues that once we know the value on the IV we can deduce the expected value on the DV from the test theory. Then we assess the congruence or incongruence of this expectation with observed values. He omits the idea that expected within-case DV values are instead established by comparison to typical IV and DV values. George, "Case Studies and Theory Development" (1982), p. 14. However, it seems to me that any such deductive exercise must rest on comparison to typical values in other cases and on expectations about the study case that are calibrated to these typical values. Hence it rests on cross-case comparison.

on the IV and DV across a range of circumstances within a case. Then the investigator assesses whether these values covary in accordance with the predictions of the test hypothesis.[26] If they covary, the test is passed. The greater the amplitude of the DV's covariance with the IV, the greater the theory's importance.

Thus to test the theory that "economic downturns cause scapegoating of ethnic minorities," we might ask whether periodic measures of scapegoating are possible at timed intervals during the Great Depression in the United States during 1929–41; and if they are, we might then ask whether scapegoating increased as the depression deepened during 1929–33, and whether scapegoating eased as the depression later eased.

Congruence procedure type 2 works best if we select cases with two characteristics: (1) many observations of values on the IV and DV are possible; and/or (2) values on the IV or DV vary sharply over time or across space (across region, institution, group, and so on) within the case.

Cases allowing many observations are better test laboratories because they allow more measures of congruence, and tests that rest on more measures are stronger.

Cases with large variation in values on the IV or DV are also good test laboratories because theories make more unique and certain predictions about these cases. For example, if values on a theory's IV vary sharply, values on its DV should also vary sharply. This sharp variance on the DV is unlikely to arise from measurement error, since the error would need to be large and to gyrate in step with the IV—an unlikely combination. The action of a third variable is also an unlikely cause, since this would require a

26. Alexander George, who coined the concept of congruence procedure, does not mention multiple within-case comparisons as a type of congruence procedure in his various writings on case studies, but his discussions of congruence procedure are consistent with the possibility of multiple observations and comparisons. See, for example, George, "Case Studies and Theory Development" (1982), pp. 13–15, and George and McKeown, "Case Studies and Theories," pp. 29–34.

third variable that gyrates in step with A and as markedly as A—an unlikely possibility, and one that is easily assessed, since such a variable will leap out from the case. Hence we can more easily rule out measurement error and omitted-variable explanations for passed tests. For parallel reasons we can also rule out these explanations for failed tests. As a result both the passage and the flunking of tests provide decisive evidence in cases with sharp variance on the IV. Passage strongly corroborates the hypothesis, failure strongly infirms it.

Congruence procedure type 2 is a within-case case study, but it shades into large-n analysis at some point as the number of within-case observations grows larger and values on variables are assigned numeric values. For example, the 1994 U.S. election is a bounded example of something more general—a parliamentary election in a democracy—hence it has aspects of a case. It also allows hundreds of observations expressed in numeric form—for example, the 435 U.S. house races. These can be studied and statistically compared. Such a study has aspects of a congruence procedure type 2 and a large-n analysis.

Case studies could, in principal, be hybrids of congruence procedure types 1 and 2. An analyst could make many observations of a case and compare these observations both to each other and to a typical value. An analyst could also select cases that offer many observations of IV and DV, extreme values on IV or DV, and large variance in these values, all at the same time.

Both types of congruence procedure can be used to test a theory's explanatory hypotheses as well as its prime hypothesis.[27] To test explanatory hypotheses, we prefer cases that permit multiple measures of, and/or display extreme or sharply varying values on, either or both variables in the tested explanatory hypothesis.

---

27. If a theory holds that "$A \rightarrow q \rightarrow B$," then "$A \rightarrow B$" is its prime hypothesis, "$A \rightarrow q$" and "$q \rightarrow B$" are its explanatory hypotheses. See "What Is a Theory?" in Chapter 1.

Process Tracing

In process tracing[28] the investigator explores the chain of events or the decision-making process by which initial case conditions are translated into case outcomes. The cause-effect link that connects independent variable and outcome is unwrapped and divided into smaller steps; then the investigator looks for observable evidence of each step.

For example, if "asteroid impacts cause mass extinctions," we should find evidence of an asteroid-caused mass killing mechanism in the sedimentary record of mass extinctions that coincide with asteroid impacts. Perhaps an impact would kill by spraying the world with molten rock, igniting global forest fires that blacken the skies in smoke, shutting out sunlight and freezing the earth. If so, the sedimentary record of mass extinctions should contain the remains of a vast continental or global molten rock shower, a layer of soot, and evidence of an abrupt mass dying of species—evidence of each step of the killing process.[29]

Likewise, if "bipolar distributions of international power cause peace," we should find, in cases of peaceful bipolarity, evidence of intervening phenomena that form the causal chains by which bipolarity causes peace. Kenneth Waltz, the prime exponent of the peacefulness of bipolarity, suggests that bipolarity causes the following pacifying phenomena: less false optimism by governments about the relative power of opponents; easier cooperation and faster learning by each side about the other, leading to thicker

28. See George and McKeown, "Case Studies and Theories," pp. 34–41; also see King, Keohane, and Verba, *Designing Social Inquiry*, pp. 226–28.
29. Evidence from the sedimentary record laid down at the time of the dinosaurs' demise 65 million years ago—which coincided with an asteroid impact—confirms these predictions. Walter Alvarez and Frank Asaro, "An Extraterrestrial Impact," *Scientific American*, October 1990, pp. 79–82. In the section "How Can Specific Events Be Explained?" in Chapter 1 I noted that this same evidence could be used to test an explanation for a specific event (the impact theory of the dinosaur's demise). This illustrates that the same evidence can test both general theories and specific explanations.

rules of the game; faster and more efficient internal and external moves by each side to balance growth in the other's power or to check the other's aggressive moves, causing deterrence; and the selection of fewer inept national political leaders.[30] A process-tracing test would look for evidence of these phenomena in cases of bipolarity (for example, the cold war, 1947–89) and, if they are found, for evidence that they stemmed from bipolarity (for example, testimony by policymakers that reveals motives and perceptions that fit this interpretation).

Evidence that a given stimulus caused a given response can be sought in the sequence and structure of events and/or in the testimony of actors explaining why they acted as they did. For example, if "commercial competition causes war," case studies of outbreaks of war should reveal pressure for war by commercially interested elites, government decisions for war should follow (not precede) this pressure, and statements in the diaries, private correspondence, memoirs, and so on of government officials should indicate that government decisions reflected this pressure. If "public relations campaigns shape public opinion," shifts in public opinion should quickly follow public relations campaigns, and interviews with citizens should reveal that they absorbed the campaign's message and changed their views in response to it.

Process predictions are often unique—no other theories predict the same pattern of events or the same actor testimony on their motives—hence process tracing often offers strong tests of a theory.[31] Hence a thorough process-trace of a single case can provide a strong test of a theory. As noted above, the investigator will still be unsure what antecedent conditions the theory may require to operate, and discovering these conditions remains an important

---

30. Kenneth N. Waltz, *Theory of International Politics* (Reading, Mass.: Addison-Wesley, 1979), pp. 161–76. My list of Waltz's hypotheses is incomplete; for the rest see ibid.
31. In other words, process tracing often provides "smoking-gun" tests—see the section "Stong/Weak Tests" in Chapter 1.

task. They can be found only by exploring other cases. Still, the validity of the theory and its ability to explain at least one case are strongly corroborated.

Theories assume many causal patterns, and we can adapt process-traces to fit these patterns. Some theories (such as, for example, the asteroid impact theory of extinctions) posit a single causal chain:

$$A \rightarrow p \rightarrow q \rightarrow r \rightarrow B$$

Some (Waltz's polarity theory of war) posit several chains:

$$
\begin{array}{c}
\rightarrow p \rightarrow \\
A \rightarrow \rightarrow q \rightarrow \rightarrow B \\
\rightarrow r \rightarrow
\end{array}
$$

A complete process-trace looks for evidence of all links in all the chains.

Case studies can assume several or all of these four formats (controlled comparison, congruence type 1, congruence type 2, and process-trace) at once. In the same study we can compare a single case to another case chosen according to Mill's method of difference or to typical conditions, we can examine it to see if within-case measures of values on the IV and DV covary over time and space, and we can study it for evidence that corroborates or infirms the theory's explanatory hypotheses.

How strong are the theory-tests that case studies pose? Scientists tested Albert Einstein's general theory of relativity with a single real-time congruence procedure type 1 case study: the observation of the May 29, 1919, solar eclipse. Einstein's theory predicted that gravity would bend the path of light toward a gravity source by a specific amount. Hence it predicted that during a solar eclipse stars near the sun would appear displaced—stars actually behind the sun would appear next to it, and stars lying next to the sun would appear farther from it—and it predicted the amount of apparent displacement. No other theory made these predictions. The passage of this one single-case-study test brought the theory wide acceptance because the tested predictions were unique— there was no plausible competing explanation for the predicted result—hence the passed test was very strong.[32] Any case study that reliably tests equally unique predictions can offer equally decisive results. Social science case studies will seldom be so decisive, but this problem stems from the messy nature of social science data and the complexity of social phenomena, not the inherent weakness of the case method.

Creating Theories with Case Studies

Case studies can serve five main purposes: testing theories, creating theories, identifying antecedent conditions, testing the importance of these antecedant conditions, and explaining cases

32. A synopsis of these events is found in Albert Einstein, *Relativity: The Special and the General Theory: A Popular Exposition*, trans. Robert W. Lawson (New York: Crown Publishers, 1961), pp. 123–32. Scientists conducted this case study in real time, studying the eclipse as it occurred, but they could just as well have studied a past eclipse if one had been photographed showing the positions of nearby stars during the eclipse.

Another decisive real-time case study from physics (also a congruence procedure type 1 study) is found in the observation of the return of Halley's comet in 1758–59, which powerfully supported Isaac Newton's theory of gravity. In 1705 astronomer Edmond Halley applied Newton's theory to predict the comet's return in 1758–59; it appeared almost exactly on schedule. Donald K. Yeomans, *Comets: A Chronological History of Observation, Science, Myth, and Folklore* (New York: John Wiley, 1991), pp. 118–19, 136. Opponents of Newton's theory "were silenced" when this and another real-time single-case-study test, the 1737 measurement of the flattening of the earth, "confirmed Newton's theory beyond a shadow of a doubt." J. Lévy, "The Solar System," in René Taton, ed., *The Beginnings of Modern Science: From 1450 to 1800* (New York: Basic Books, 1964), p. 438.

of intrinsic importance.[33] The previous section discussed theory testing. This section covers theory-making.[34]

To infer new theories from cases we start by searching cases for associations between phenomena and for testimony by people who directly experienced the case (actors in the case, for instance) on their motives and beliefs about the case. These associations and participant accounts offer clues on cause and effect. Then we ask: "Of what more general phenomena are these specific causes and effects examples?" Once candidate causes and effects are framed in general terms the investigator has theories that can be tested against other evidence and applied to other cases.

Investigators can use four basic methods to infer theories from case studies: controlled comparison, congruence procedures, and process tracing (all covered in the previous section) and the Delphi method. Controlled comparison compares observations across cases to infer theories. Congruence procedure and process tracing deduce theories from observations within cases. The Delphi method consults the views of case participants.

Controlled Comparison

In a controlled comparison the investigator infers hypotheses from contrasts or similarities in aspects of several cases, following Mill's methods of difference and agreement. In the method of difference the investigator explores several cases with similar characteristics and different values on the study variable (the variable whose causes or effects we seek to discover), looking for

33. These purposes overlap and several (for example, explaining cases, creating theories and testing theories; identifying and testing antecedent conditions) often can and should be pursued simultaneously. For another typology of case-study formats see note 17.
34. Theory-making case studies are also called "heuristic," "hypothesis-generating," and "exploratory" case studies. Eckstein, "Case Study and Theory," pp. 104–8; Lijphart, "Comparative Politics and the Comparative Method," p. 692; Yin, *Case Study Research*, pp. 1, 3–4.

other differences between the cases. These other cross-case differences are nominated as possible causes of the study variable (if we seek to discover its causes) or possible effects (if we seek its effects). The investigator picks similar cases to reduce the number of candidate causes or effects that emerge: the more similar the cases, the fewer the candidate causes. This makes the real cause easier to spot.[35]

In the method of agreement the analyst explores cases with different characteristics and similar values on the study variable, looking for other similarities between the cases. These similarities are nominated as candidate causes or effects of the variable.

The method of difference is preferred when the characteristics of available cases are homogeneous (most things about most cases are quite similar). The method of agreement is preferred when the characteristics of available cases are heterogeneous (most things about most cases are different).

Congruence Procedures

When using congruence procedures, the investigator explores a case looking for within-case correlation between the study variable and other phenomena. These phenomena are nominated as possible independent variables in new hypotheses (if we seek to establish the study variable's causes) or as possible dependent variables (if we seek to establish its effects). Three specific formats are used.

1. The investigator "examines the outliers," exploring cases that are poorly explained by known causes, on the assumption that unknown causes explain their outcomes. Specifically, the investigator looks for cases where the study phenomenon is present but its known causes are absent. Still-undiscovered causes must explain the phenomenon. These causal phenomena should be ob-

35. For examples of method-of-difference theory making, see note 25 to Chapter 1.

served in above-normal amounts in the case and should be observed covarying with the study variable.[36]

2. The investigator selects cases with extreme high or low values on the study variable, and explores them looking for other phenomena that are present in above-normal or below-normal amounts. When the study phenomenon is present in abundance, its causes and effects should also be present in unusual abundance and so should stand out against the case background. When the study phenomenon is absent, its causes and effects should also be prominent by their absence.

3. The investigator selects cases with extreme within-case variance on the dependent variable, and explores them looking for phenomena that covary with the study variable. If values on the study variable vary sharply, its causes and effects should also vary sharply, standing out against the more static case background.

Process Tracing

The investigator traces backward the causal process that produces the case outcome, at each stage inferring from the context what caused each cause. If this backward process-trace succeeds, it leads the investigator back to a prime cause.

The Delphi Method

In the Delphi method the investigator mines the views of case participants or others who experienced the case for hypotheses. Those who experience a case often observe important unrecorded data that is lost to later investigators. The investigator uses their

---

36. Studies of outlier cases are also known as "deviant" case studies. Lijphart, "Comparative Politics and the Comparative Method," pp. 692–93. The logic of studying outliers follows the logic of John Stuart Mill's "method of residues"; on this method see Mill, *A System of Logic*, pp. 397–98.

memories and judgments to infer hypotheses that could not be made from direct observation alone.[37]

Inferring Antecedent Conditions from Case Studies

As noted above, a weakness of the single-case study is its concealment of theories' antecedent conditions—the background conditions required for theories to operate or that magnify their action. However, one can uncover these background conditions by examining selected new cases.

Four methods of inferring antecedent conditions are most useful. (These methods parallel the four methods of inferring theories, outlined above.)

1. *Controlled comparison.* The investigator uses Mill's method of difference to infer antecedent conditions from contrasts or similarities in the characteristics of several cases.[38] Specifically, the investigator selects and examines new cases that resemble previously studied cases in all ways—except their value on the dependent variable. For example, if previously examined cases had high values on the independent and dependent variables, we would now examine cases with high values on the IV, low values on the DV, and a close resemblance to the previously examined cases in other regards. Thus if the hypothesis that "economic downturns cause trade closure" has been tested using Europe 1929–39 as a case (high values on IV and DV), we would next look for cases when downturns occurred without closure. If we can find no high-IV–low-DV cases, this suggests that the conditions required for the theory's operation are abundant, and the theory

37. For an example of Delphi-method theory-making see Chapter 1, note 27. The Delphi method does not have much stature as a method for testing theories or explanations partly because the Delphi expert's discovery process cannot be replicated.
38. The method of agreement is too weak to bother with.

has broad applicability (or "external validity"). If we find such cases, we inspect them for points of difference with previously examined cases. Important antecedent conditions will appear as these points of cross-case difference.

2. *Congruence procedures.* The investigator measures the gap between the predicted and observed values on the dependent variable in a case and then looks for correlations between the size of the gap and values on other phenomena within the case. The investigator then nominates phenomena that correlate with the gap (that are scarce when the value on the DV is lower than the IV value warrants and are abundant when the DV value is higher than the IV value warrants) as possible antecedent conditions. Two formats are used.

The investigator can examine the outliers—those cases where the theory's posited cause is present but its predicted effect is absent. If we assume the theory is valid, this pattern indicates that an important antecedent condition is also notably absent. The missing antecedent condition can be identified among conditions that are often present but are absent in the outlier case.

The investigator can also explore cases with large within-case variance in the value on the dependent variable and constant high values on the independent variable. This pattern suggests that an important antecedent condition varies within the case.[39] It should announce itself as a factor that covaries with the DV.

3. *Process tracing.* The investigator traces backward the causal process by which the case outcome was produced, at each stage attempting to infer from the context what antecedent conditions the process requires.

4. *The Delphi method.* The investigator mines the views of case participants or others who experienced the case for possible

---

39. This pattern may also occur solely because of variance in the value of other variables that cause the DV.

antecedent conditions. They may have observed in person telltale dynamics that cannot be observed in retrospect by nonparticipants.

Testing Antecedent Conditions with Case Studies

Antecedent conditions, like hypotheses, should be tested before they are lent credibility. Like hypotheses they can be tested three ways: controlled comparison, congruence procedures, and process tracing.

1. *Controlled comparison.* The investigator explores paired observations in two or more cases, asking if values on the pairs are congruent or incongruent with the premise that the antecedent condition magnifies the causal action of the independent variable on the dependent variable. For example, if values on the condition variable are higher in case A than case B, values on the dependent variable should also be higher, relative to values on the independent variable, in case A than B. If possible, the investigator selects cases according to an adaption of Mill's criteria for the method of difference: cases should have similar general characteristics, similar values on the IV, and different outcomes. If the condition variable (CV) has an impact, its values should covary with values on the DV.

2. *Congruence procedures.* Two congruence procedures are most useful for testing antecedent conditions. First, the investigator studies cases with extreme (high or low) values on the condition variable and a value greater than zero on the independent variable. A very high value on the CV should multiply the effects of the IV on the intervening variables (IntVs) and DV, moving their values above predicted ranges (with "predicted" meaning the value predicted by the test theory in light of the value on the IV in the case). A very low value on the CV should diminish the IV's

impact on IntVs and DV, lowering their values below predicted ranges.[40] Second, the investigator studies cases with large within-case variance on the value of the CV and little or no within-case variance on the IV. If the CV is important, the DV's value should covary with it.[41]

3. *Process tracing.* The investigator explores the chain of events or the decision-making process by which initial case conditions are translated into case outcomes. Antecedent conditions will leave footprints in this process: actors may refer to their importance and events will occur in a sequence that follows their appearance and disappearance.

Explaining Cases

As noted in Chapter 1,[42] explanations for specific cases[43] are assessed by answering four questions:

1. Does the explanation exemplify a valid general theory (a covering law)? The specific explanation must exemplify a valid covering law. An explanation that rests on a false general theory falls.

2. Is the covering law's causal phenomenon present in the case? The explanation's causal phenomenon must be present in the case.

40. This test assumes that the catalytic effect of the CV is linear, expanding continuously as the value on the CV rises. It is inappropriate if logic suggests that the impact of the CV hits a threshold at some point, flattening out when the value of the CV rises above a certain level.

41. These two methods parallel the methods of congruence procedure type 1 (comparison to typical values) and type 2 (multiple within-case comparisons). See the discussion of congruence procedures in the section "Testing Theories with Case Studies" in this chapter.

42. See "How Can Specific Events Be Explained?" in Chapter 1.

43. Case-explaining studies are also called "explanatory," "interpretive," and "disciplined-configurative" case studies. Yin, *Case Study Research*, p. 5; Lijphart, "Comparative Politics and the Comparative Method," p. 692; Eckstein, "Case Study and Theory," pp. 99–104.

If not, the explanation falls. (Even if *A* is a confirmed cause of *B*, it cannot explain instances of *B* that occur when *A* is absent.)

3. Are the covering law's antecedent conditions met in the case? Theories cannot explain the outcomes of cases that omit their necessary antecedent conditions.

4. Are the covering law's intervening phenomena observed in the case? The phenomena that link the covering law's posited cause and effect should be evident in the case and appear in the proper order and location.

The logic of case-explaining parallels that of a pathologist doing an autopsy or a detective solving a crime. Specific explanations of the death (or crime) are evaluated by asking if they rest on a valid covering law, if the conditions for that covering law's operation— its cause and required antecedent conditions—are observed in the case at hand, and if telltale phenomena that signal its inner workings are also observed. A case-explaining inquiry does not test theories, although the evidence collected could also be used to check a theory's validity.

Political scientists seldom do case-explaining case studies, partly because they define the task of case-explaining as the domain of historians; however, historians often explain cases in a softer way than political scientists would. Their explanations are left vague, and the predictions they infer from these explanations are left unspecified, hence the meaning of their evidence is often ambiguous. The general theories that underlie their explanations are often deeply buried. As a result their explanations are hard to interpret and evaluate. This leaves wide latitude for political scientists to contribute to discussion of historical explanation.

Strong vs. Weak Tests; Predictions and Tests

Strong tests are better than weak tests, and the results of strong tests carry more weight than the results of weak tests.

As noted in the section "Strong vs. Weak Tests" in Chapter 1, a strong test is one whose outcome is unlikely to result from any factor except the operation or failure of the theory. Strong tests evaluate predictions that are *certain* and *unique*. A *certain* prediction is an unequivocal forecast. The more certain the prediction, the stronger the test. A *unique* prediction is a forecast not made by other known theories. The more unique the prediction, the stronger the test.

When testing a theory, the investigator should select cases that enable the most strong tests. This calls for selection of cases about which the test theory makes certain or unique predictions (or both).

In writing up cases, authors should explain and justify the predictions they test. Interpretive disputes about case studies often arise from disputes about the fairness of the predictions tested. These disputes can be rationalized by offering a few words on why the prediction seems fair.

Authors should also comment on the strength of the tests performed. How unique and how certain were the predictions tested? Were the tests of the smoking-gun, hoop, doubly-decisive, or straw-in-the-wind variety?[44]

Interpreting Contradictory Results

What should investigators do when tests produce contrary results—when theories pass some tests and flunk others? Answer: investigate further. Five procedures are appropriate:

1. Infer and test additional predictions, with a special eye toward finding "hoop" and "smoking-gun" tests. Such additional tests may resolve the confusion.

2. Double-check the accuracy of data used for past tests. Some

44. On these types of test see the section "Strong vs. Weak Tests" in Chapter 1.

may be wrong. If so, an unambiguous result may emerge from double-checking: all tests may now be passed or flunked.

3. Reconsider the predictions you inferred from the theory. Were they fair? Sometimes false flunks (or false passes) are reported because false predictions are tested.

4. Replicate your tests using new cases. Replication may produce more consistent results.

5. Repair the theory in ways that enable it to pass flunked tests, by limiting the scope of its claims or by removing flunked explanatory hypotheses. This can salvage a damaged theory (although the salvaged product is now a different, narrower theory).

Case-Selection Criteria

Practitioners of case studies have produced neither a comprehensive catalog of possible case-study research designs[45] nor a comprehensive list of case-selection methods. Accordingly, I have made my own list of useful case-selection criteria.[46] My list (of eleven criteria) does not exhaust the logical possibilities, but it includes all that seem strong to me. Specifically, I argue that the following case attributes are possible reasons for case selection: (1) data richness; (2) extreme values on the independent variable, dependent variable, or condition variable; (3) large within-case variance in values on the independent, dependent, or condition variables; (4) divergence of predictions made of the case by competing theories; (5) the resemblance of case background conditions to the conditions of current policy problems; (6) prototypicality of case background conditions; (7) appropriateness for controlled comparison with other cases (mainly using Mill's method of difference); (8) outlier character; (9) intrinsic impor-

45. Noting this failure is Yin, *Case Study Research*, p. 18.
46. These criteria evolved from discussions with Andy Bennett, Tom Christensen, Chaim Kaufmann, Jack Snyder, and Steve Walt and include their ideas.

tance; (10) appropriateness for replication of previous tests; and (11) appropriateness for performing a previously omitted type of test.

This list reflects two general criteria for case selection:

First, investigators should select cases that best serve the purpose of their inquiry. As noted earlier, there are five purposes for case studies: testing theories, creating theories, identifying possible antecedent conditions that theories require to operate, testing the importance of these antecedent conditions, and explaining cases of intrinsic importance. The selection criterion that is most appropriate differs from purpose to purpose, hence investigators should be clear in their purpose before they select cases.[47] Some of the following selection criteria are appropriate for most purposes, but some serve only one or two purposes. Hence investigators should take care to match criteria and purpose. (See the table at the end of this chapter, for a summary of matches and mismatches between mission and case-selection criteria.)

Case-selection criteria should therefore differ with the stage at which the investigation stands. Investigators first seek to infer theories, then to test theories, then to test their range (or "external validity") by inferring and testing antecedent conditions. Rules for case selection vary across these tasks, and hence vary with the stage of the inquiry.

Second, when testing theories investigators should select cases to maximize the strength and number of tests they let the investigator perform. The best case selection allows the most strong tests (tests of predictions that are certain and/or unique) with the least research effort.[48]

---

47. This means you cannot know what cases are best to select until you frame your questions. Decisions on case selection are premature before you know what you want to know.

48. Some of what follows repeats remarks made earlier on inferring and testing theories and antecedent conditions, since methods of case selection are an aspect of general methods of inquiry.

1. *Select data-rich cases.* We learn more from case studies that let us answer more questions about the case. The more data we have the more questions we can answer. Hence more tests are possible, hence data-rich cases are preferred, other things being equal.[49]

Selecting cases for data-richness is especially appropriate if you plan to infer or test theories using process tracing, since process tracing requires a great deal of data.

Data richness can take several forms. Abundant archival data may be available. Participants in the case may be alive and available for interviews. Other scholars may have studied the case for their own purposes and done much of the legwork for you.

2. *Select cases with extreme (high or low) values on the independent variable (IV), the dependent variable (DV), or the condition variable (CV).*[50] Under this method we select cases in which the study variable (the variable whose causes or effects we seek to establish) is present in unusually large quantities or unusually small quantities.[51]

To test a theory, select cases with extreme values on the independent variable. Such cases offer strong tests because the theory's predictions about the case are certain and unique (as noted above in this chapter.)

It is often argued that one should select cases that are representative or typical of the universe of cases. The "extreme value on the IV" method of case selection argues the opposite, that cases that are atypical in their endowment with the independent variable teach us the most.[52]

---

49. Yin, *Case Study Research*, p. 40, concurs.
50. Recommending this selection criteria is Eckstein, "Case Study and Theory," pp. 119–20.
51. This "extreme value" method of case selection is closely akin to method 7, controlled comparison. The difference is only that with method 7 cases are selected to ease explicit cross-case comparisons, whereas here cases are selected to ease implicit comparisons to normal conditions. Such comparisons are clearest if within-case values on IV and DV contrast clearly with their normal values.
52. Thus I chose the 1914 case to test offense-defense theory (which posits that

Some also argue that selecting cases for extreme values on the IV sets up weak tests because passage of the test is likely: high IV values should elevate some DV values even if the theory operates only weakly, hence the test is easy to pass. This view rests, however, on a false definition of "strong test." A strong test is one whose outcome is unlikely to result from any factor other than the operation or failure of the theory. According to this definition, a test using a case selected for extreme value on the IV is a strong test. We should expect extreme results in such a test.[53] If they occur, these extreme results are unlikely to stem from other factors. If they do not occur, this is unlikely to stem from any cause other than the theory's failure. Hence cases with extreme IV values are laboratories for strong tests.

To make a theory, select cases with extreme values on the study variable. If values on the study variable are very high, its causes (or effects, if these are sought) should be present in unusual abundance, hence these causes (or effects) should stand out against the background of the case more clearly. This makes them easier to

---

war is more likely when conquest is believed easy) partly because 1914 was the heyday of the "cult of the offensive," a remarkable European elite belief that conquest was easy. Shortly before 1914 this belief reached heights never seen before or since. Because it was extreme it should have had extreme effects, if it ever has any effects. Hence these effects should have been clearly visible in 1914, standing out starkly from the European political landscape, and should have appeared in quantities unlikely to be produced by measurement error or by the action of other causes.

The predictions of offense-defense theory in 1914 therefore are both certain and unique. The predicted effects are too large to ascribe to measurement error or to other causes (hence the predictions are unique). The absence of these effects likewise could not be plausibly blamed on measurement error or the overriding effects of other phenomena, since these could not mask or override such large effects (hence the predictions are certain). Hence the test posed by the 1914 case is strong. Offense-defense theory would be strongly corroborated by passing it and badly damaged by flunking it. See Van Evera, *Causes of War* (Ithaca, N.Y.: Cornell University Press, in press), vol. 1, chap. 7.

53. I assume there is no threshold effect, that the impact of the IV on the DV does not peter out above a certain threshold. With threshold effects this selection criteria is less useful.

spot. Likewise, if values on the study variable are unusually low its causes (or effects) should be made more striking by their absence.

To infer antecedent conditions, select cases with extreme and opposite values on the IV and DV—specifically, with very high values on IVs and very low values on DVs. These are cases where the theory's posited cause is abundantly present but the predicted effect is notably absent. For example, to infer conditions required for literacy to cause democracy, we should select highly literate societies with authoritarian regimes. To infer conditions required for economic depression to cause war, we should select cases where deep depressions occurred but no war resulted, and so on. Such a pattern indicates that an important antecedent condition is also notably absent. The missing condition can be identified among conditions that are normally present but are absent in the studied case.[54]

To test a candidate antecedent condition (a condition that a theory requires to operate or that magnifies its action), select cases with extreme values on the condition variable. A high value on the CV should multiply the effect of the IV on intervening variables (IntVs) and DV. A low value on the CV should leave the IV with little impact on IntVs and DV. In both instances the predicted results are pronounced and hence less likely to arise from measurement error or the actions of a third variable.[55]

54. Under the selection methods discussed in the previous four paragraphs, cases are chosen to highlight the contrast between observed and normal values on the IV and DV. Here, in contrast, cases are chosen to highlight the contrast between observed values on IV and DV. Sharp contrasts are sought in both cases, although the sought contrasts differ in nature.

55. This selection strategy needs adjustment if the impact of antecedent conditions follows sharp thresholds—if the IV requires some value on the CV to cause the DV but further increases in the value on the CV have no effects. Thus seed and fertilizer cannot cause grass to grow without some accompanying rainfall, but beyond a certain point enough rain is enough, and too much will drown the grass. In such cases we should select cases for very low values on the CV and test the prediction that the IV should lack causal power in such cases. Selecting cases

3. *Select cases with large within-case variance in the value on the independent variable, dependent variable, or condition variable* across time or space.[56]

To test a theory, select cases with large within-case variance in the value on the independent variable. Theories make predictions about the impact of variance in the value on the IV, hence variance in the IV's value generates predictions, hence the more within-case variance in the IV's value, the more predictions we have to test. Such variance takes the form of diachronic or synchronous change in the value on the IV—that is, change over time within the period covered by the case, or diversity on the value of the IV across regions, groups, organizations, or individuals present in the case.

Selecting cases for within-case IV-value variance is especially appropriate if you plan to use a congruence procedure type 2 for testing, since type 2 congruence procedures rely on observing within-case variance.

To make a theory, select cases with large within-case variance in the value on the study variable. The causes and effects of the study variable should also vary widely in such a case, in step with the study variable. This makes them easier to spot against the case background. Candidate causes and effects will announce themselves as case characteristics that vary with the SV's value—that is, as factors present when the value on the SV is high, missing when it is low.

To infer a theory's antecedent conditions, select cases with large within-case variance in the value on the DV and constant high values on the IV. Such a case contains some observations where the relative value on the IV and DV match the theory's predictions (high on IV and DV), and some where it does not (high

---

with very large values on the CV is unfruitful, since very large values predict the same results as moderate values.

56. Obliquely recommending this selection criteria is Eckstein, "Case Study and Theory," pp. 119, 126.

on IV, low on DV). Candidate antecedent conditions will announce themselves as factors that are more abundant when relative values match predictions—that is, when DV values are higher.

To test a candidate antecedent condition, select cases with large within-case variance on the value of the CV. If the CV is important, the DV's value should be higher, relative to the IV's value, when the CV is abundant than when it is scarce.

4. *Select cases about which competing theories make opposite predictions.* This selection method is appropriate if you are more interested in testing the relative power of the two theories than testing a theory against the null hypothesis (that is, if you prefer to arrange a Lakatosian "three-cornered fight" over a "two-cornered fight").[57]

If you are testing the relative power of two theories, choose cases about which they make opposite predictions, for instance, a case with opposite within-case variance in the values on the two IVs (values on one IV fall over time and values on the other rise over time). The DV should covary with the stronger IV.

If you are testing the relative power of two antecedent conditions, choose cases where the IV is present and the CVs show opposite within-case variance (e.g., values on one CV fall over time, values on the other rise over time). The DV should covary with the stronger CV.

For best results, select cases that allow tests of predictions that are unique and certain as well as opposite.

5. *Select cases that resemble current situations of policy concern.*[58] A theory inferred from or tested in a case that resembles a second case will more often "travel" to that second case—that is, operate in the second case as well. Hence policy prescriptions deduced from the first case can be more safely applied to the second.

---

57. On two- and three-cornered fights see note 43 to Chapter 1.
58. Jack Snyder recommends this criterion.

Scholars interested in offering policy prescriptions should therefore study cases whose background characteristics parallel the characteristics of current or future policy problems.

A study of health policy in Minnesota yields more reliable prescriptions for health policy in Wisconsin than a study of health policy in Burkina Faso. Theories that operate in Burkina Faso may well require conditions absent in Wisconsin, hence prescriptions deduced from these theories will prove unsound in Wisconsin. This is less likely of theories that operate in Minnesota, since Minnesota and Wisconsin are similar in many ways.

6. *Select cases with prototypical background characteristics.* One might select cases with average or typical background conditions, on the grounds that theories that pass the tests these cases pose are more likely to "travel" well, applying widely to other cases.

This selection method is sometimes appropriate but is overused. If one is seeking theories with wide applicability, it is often more appropriate to follow selection method 5, "select cases that resemble current situations of policy concern," since that method offers a better guarantee that corroborated theories will apply to other important situations. Method 6 selects theories that apply widely; method 5 selects theories that less widely overall but more widely to important circumstances. The latter goal is often more important.

7. *Select cases that are well matched for controlled cross-case comparisons.* One can select cases to allow their pairing for controlled comparison, that is, for the method of difference (cases have similar characteristics and different values on the study variable) or the method of agreement (cases have different characteristics and similar values on the study variable). The method of difference, being the stronger of the two, is usually preferred.

Controlled-comparison criteria can be applied to select one or more cases. A single case can be selected with an eye to comparing it to existing case studies that others have already researched and written. Specifically, if we plan to perform a method-of-difference comparison, we select a new case whose characteristics resemble those of an already-studied case but which has different values on the study variable. Multiple cases can be selected with an eye to comparing them (in other words, if we plan to perform a method-of-difference comparison, we select cases with similar characteristics and diverse study-variable values) or with existing cases (we select cases with characteristics similar to those of an already-studied case but with different values on the study variable).

To test a theory using a controlled-comparison method, select cases with similar characteristics and different values on the study variable (that is, select for the method of difference). The theory passes the test if study reveals that values on IV and DV correspond across the cases. If, for example, the IV has a higher value in case 1 than case 2, the DV should also have a higher value in case 1 than case 2.

Remember, however, the method of difference is a fairly weak instrument for theory testing (and the method of agreement is even weaker). Hence other selection criteria should have higher priority for theory-testers.

To make a theory, select cases with similar characteristics and different values on the study variable (for method-of-difference comparison) or cases with different characteristics and similar values on the study variable (for method-of-agreement comparison).

Candidate causes or effects will announce themselves as differences in the characteristics of the compared cases when the method of difference is used. They announce themselves as similarities in the characteristics of compared cases when the method of agreement is used.

The method of difference is preferred when the characteristics of available cases are quite homogeneous (most things about most cases are similar). The method of agreement is preferred when the characteristics of available cases are quite heterogeneous (most things about most cases are different).

To infer antecedent conditions, select cases using variants of the method of difference or the method of agreement.

For the method of difference, choose cases with (1) similar values on the IV; (2) similar case characteristics; and (3) different values on the DV. Candidate antecedent conditions will announce themselves as differences in the characteristics of the compared cases.

For the method of agreement, choose cases with (1) similar values on the IV; (2) different case characteristics; and (3) similar values on the DV. Candidate antecedent conditions will announce themselves as similarities in the characteristics of the compared cases.

When testing a candidate antecedent condition, select cases with (1) similar values on the IV and (2) different values on the DV. The condition passes its test if values on the CV correspond with values on the DV across cases.

8. *Select outlier cases.* Here the investigator selects cases that are poorly explained by existing theories, on the assumption that unknown causes explain their outcomes and can be identified by examining the case. We select cases where the values on the dependent variable are high and its known causes are absent. Candidate new causes will announce themselves as unusual characteristics of these cases and as characteristics that correspond with the DV within the case.

To make a theory, select cases where the DV's known causes are scarce yet the DV is abundantly present. This suggests that unknown causes are operating in the case and that study of the case may reveal them.

To infer an antecedent condition, select cases where the DV's known causes are abundant yet the DV is scarce or absent. This suggests that unknown antecedent conditions are absent in the case, and that study of the case may identify them.

9. *Select cases of intrinsic importance.* Selecting cases of intrinsic human or historical importance (World War I, World War II, the

Holocaust) is appropriate if our object is to explain the course of history. We select such cases with a nod to their data-richness (there is little point in studying cases where the record is too thin to answer our questions), but mainly in accord with the magnitude of their human consequences.

10. *Select for test replication.* Thorough theory testing requires repeating initial tests to corroborate their results. When doing this, we choose cases for their appropriateness as laboratories to replicate previous tests.[59] This approach considers multiple cases as multiple experiments. Test replication, not cross-case comparison, is the goal of later studies in the series.

A replication can be exact or inexact (a "quasi-replication"). An exact replication repeats a previous test exactly with a similar case. A quasi-replication (which is far more common) repeats a previous test with some alteration to the research design.[60] Cases are selected by means of the same selection criteria used to select the case(s) for the test being replicated.

11. *Select for previously omitted types of tests.* If a theory has already faced one kind of test, it may now be appropriate to subject it to a another kind of test. For example, if a theory has already faced congruence procedure case-study tests it may now be appropriate to subject it to a process-tracing case-study test. We select such cases for their utility as process-tracing test beds.

Can the investigator test a theory with the same case from which it was inferred? As I noted in Chapter 1,[61] this practice is criticized on grounds that such tests lack integrity. The criticism rests on a preference for blind testing. The assumption is that data not used to infer a theory are less well known to an investigator

59. Making this point is Yin, *Case Study Research*, pp. 45–50.
60. On quasi-replication see Edward S. Balian, *How to Design, Analyze, and Write Doctoral or Masters Research*, 2d ed. (Lanham, Md.: University Press of America, 1988), pp. 12–13.
61. See the discussion of blind testing (item 3) in the section "Methodology Myths" in Chapter 1.

than used data, hence the investigator using unused data is less tempted to sample the data selectively.

Prohibiting the reuse of theory-inspiring cases for theory testing is not feasible in practice, however, and would cause a loss of good evidence. Other barriers against test-fudging—for example, infusing social science professions with high standards of honesty—are more practical.

Table 1, below, summarizes matches and mismatches of study missions and case-selection criteria.

Table 1. Eleven Case Selection Criteria: When Is Each Appropriate?

Case selection criteria	When testing theories?	When inferring theories?	When inferring antecedent conditions?	When testing antecedent conditions?	When studying cases of intrinsic importance?
1. Data richness	Yes	Yes	Yes	Yes	Maybe
2. Extreme values on IV, DV, or CV	Yes (on IV)	Yes (on SV)	Yes (high on IV, low on DV)	Yes (on CV)	No
3. Large within-case variance in values on IV, DV, or CV	Yes (on IV)	Yes (on SV)	Yes (on DV)	Yes (on CV)	No
4. Competing theories make divergent predictions about the case	Yes	No	No	Yes	No
5. Resemblance to current policy-problem cases	Yes	Yes	Yes	Yes	No
6. Prototypical case characteristics	Sometimes	Sometimes	No	No	No
7. Matched for cross-case controlled comparison (namely, method of difference or agreement)	Seldom	Yes	Yes	Seldom	No
8. Outcome unexplained by other theories (thus, an "outlier" case)	No	Yes	Yes	No	No
9. Intrinsic importance	No	No	No	No	Yes
10. Good case for replicating previous tests	Yes	No	No	Yes	No
11. Allows a new type of test	Yes	No	No	Yes	No

CHAPTER 3

What Is a
Political Science
Dissertation?

Dissertations in political science[1] can perform seven principal missions. This gives rise to seven types of dissertation, one for each mission. Most dissertations perform several of these missions, and thus are hybrids, but it is still useful to consider possible ideal-type dissertations.

1. A *theory-proposing* dissertation advances new hypotheses. A deductive argument for these hypotheses is advanced. Examples may be offered to illustrate these hypotheses and to demonstrate their plausibility, but strong empirical tests are not performed.[2]

---

1. As my examples suggest, what follows was drafted for students in the subfield of international relations and security affairs. It should also apply to other political science subfields, however, with the exception of political philosophy. Apologies to those in other subfields for my IR-centric examples.

2. Examples of theory-proposing works include Robert Jervis, *Perception and Misperception in International Politics* (Princeton: Princeton University Press, 1976); Robert Jervis, "Cooperation Under the Security Dilemma," *World Politics* 30 (January 1978): 167–214; Kenneth N. Waltz, *Theory of International Politics* (Reading, Mass.: Addison-Wesley, 1979); Geoffrey Blainey, *The Causes of War*, 3d ed. (New York: Free Press, 1988); Thomas C. Schelling, *Arms and Influence* (New Haven: Yale University Press, 1966); Thomas C. Schelling, *The Strategy of Conflict* (New York: Oxford University Press, 1960); Robert Axelrod, *The Evolution of Cooperation* (New York: Basic Books, 1984); Carl von Clausewitz, *On War* (Prince-

2. A *theory-testing* dissertation uses empirical evidence to evaluate existing theories. This evidence can take the form of large-*n* analysis, case studies, or both.[3]

Many dissertations are a blend of type 1 and 2. They do some theory-proposing and some theory-testing.[4] However, a good thesis can focus exclusively on proposing theory, or on testing theory, as long as it contributes useful knowledge.

3. A *literature-assessing* (or "stock-taking") dissertation summarizes and evaluates existing theoretical and empirical literature on a subject. It asks whether existing theories are valuable and existing tests are persuasive and complete.[5]

---

ton: Princeton University Press, 1976); and Hans J. Morgenthau, *Politics Among Nations*, 5th ed. (New York: Knopf, 1973). Note: hypotheses may be developed by deduction (Schelling) or by induction (Clausewitz), or both.

3. Examples of works that focus on theory-testing include Richard K. Betts, *Nuclear Blackmail and Nuclear Balance* (Washington, D.C.: Brookings Institution, 1987); Steve Chan, "Mirror, Mirror on the Wall . . . Are the Freer Countries More Pacific?" *Journal of Conflict Resolution* 28 (December 1984): 617–48; Erich Weede, "Democracy and War Involvement," ibid., pp. 649–64; and Zeev Maoz and Bruce Russett, "Normative and Structural Causes of Democratic Peace, 1946–1986," *American Political Science Review* 87 (September 1993): 624–38.

4. Works that both propose and test theories include Barry R. Posen, *The Sources of Military Doctrine: France, Britain, and Germany Between the World Wars* (Ithaca: Cornell University Press, 1984); Stephen M. Walt, *The Origins of Alliances* (Ithaca: Cornell University Press, 1987); Jack Snyder, *Myths of Empire* (Ithaca: Cornell University Press, 1991); Jack Snyder, *Ideology of the Offensive: Military Decision Making and the Disasters of 1914* (Ithaca: Cornell University Press, 1984); and John J. Mearsheimer, *Conventional Deterrence* (Ithaca: Cornell University Press, 1983). Note: such works often begin as theory-testing projects; the authors begin by testing others' theories, and develop their own theories in midstream. This reflects the great difficulty of creating theory from a standing start. I advise students not to try it. Instead, test someone else's theory. Creative lightning may strike you while you're at it but if it doesn't you can still produce a good thesis.

5. Examples of literature-assessing works include Kenneth N. Waltz, *Man, the State, and War* (New York: Columbia University Press, 1959); Benjamin Cohen, *The Question of Imperialism* (New York: Basic Books, 1973); Jack Levy, "The Causes of War: A Review of Theories and Evidence," in Philip E. Tetlock, Jo L. Husbands, Robert Jervis, Paul C. Stern, and Charles Tilly, eds., *Behavior, Society, and Nuclear War* (New York: Oxford University Press, 1989), 1:209–333; and Robert Gilpin with Jean M. Gilpin, *The Political Economy of International Relations* (Princeton: Princeton University Press, 1987).

4. A *policy-evaluative* or *policy-prescriptive* dissertation evaluates current or future public policies or policy proposals. Are the factual and theoretical premises of the proponents and opponents of proposed policies valid or invalid? Will the policy produce the results that its proponents promise?

It is often said that policy-prescriptive work is not theoretical. The opposite is true. All policy proposals rest on forecasts about the effects of policies. These forecasts rest in turn on implicit or explicit theoretical assumptions about the laws of social and political motion. Hence all evaluation of public policy requires the framing and evaluation of theory, hence it is fundamentally theoretical.[6]

Policy prescriptive work can focus on evaluating a particular policy; on evaluating competing solutions to a given problem; or on the policy implications of a political or technical development (such as, for example, the nuclear revolution or the collapse of the Soviet empire).

5. A *historical explanatory* dissertation uses theory (academically recognized theory, folk theory, or "common sense" deduction) to explain the causes, pattern, or consequences of historical cases.

6. Examples of policy prescriptive work include Jerome Slater, "Dominos in Central America: Will They Fall? Does It Matter?" *International Security* 12 (Fall 1987): 105–34; Charles L. Glaser, *Analyzing Strategic Nuclear Policy* (Princeton: Princeton University Press, 1990); Robert Jervis, *The Illogic of American Nuclear Strategy* (Ithaca: Cornell University Press, 1984); Shai Feldman, *Israeli Nuclear Deterrence* (New York: Columbia University Press, 1982); Robert Art, "A Defensible Defense: America's Grand Strategy after the Cold War," *International Security* 15 (Spring 1991): 5–53; Barry Posen, "Inadvertent Nuclear War? Escalation and NATO's Northern Flank," ibid., vol. 7 (Fall 1982): 28–54; John J. Mearsheimer, "A Strategic Misstep: The Maritime Strategy and Deterrence in Europe," ibid., vol. 11 (Fall 1986): 3–57; Samuel Huntington, "Conventional Deterrence and Conventional Retaliation in Europe," ibid., vol. 8 (Winter 1983–84): 32–56; Joshua Epstein, "Soviet Vulnerabilities and the RDF Deterrent," ibid., vol. 6 (Fall 1981): 126–58; and Albert Wohlstetter, "The Delicate Balance of Terror," *Foreign Affairs* 37 (January 1959). Nicely evaluating a Soviet policy is Richard Ned Lebow, "The Soviet Offensive in Europe: The Schlieffen Plan Revisited?" *International Security* 9 (Spring 1985): 44–78.

Such works often provide a good deal of description but focus on explaining what is described.[7]

6. A *historical evaluative* dissertation evaluates the factual and theoretical beliefs that guided official or unofficial policy actors, and/or evaluates the consequences of the policies they pursued.[8]

Dissertations of types 5 and 6 are rare and little admired in political science. This reflects a general bias in the field favoring the creation and testing of theory over the application of theory. However, this bias is misguided. If theories are never applied,

7. Examples of historical explanatory works are James C. Thompson, "How Could Vietnam Happen? An Autopsy," in Morton H. Halperin and Arnold Kanter, eds., *Readings in American Foreign Policy: A Bureaucratic Perspective* (Boston: Little, Brown, 1973), pp. 98–110; Leslie H. Gelb with Richard K. Betts, *The Irony of Vietnam: The System Worked* (Washington, D.C.: Brookings Institution, 1979); Larry Berman, *Planning a Tragedy: The Americanization of the War in Vietnam* (New York: W. W. Norton, 1982); John Lewis Gaddis, "The Long Peace: Elements of Stability in the Postwar International System," *International Security* 10 (Spring 1986): 99–142; Arthur Schlesinger, Jr., "Origins of the Cold War," *Foreign Affairs* 46 (October 1967): 22–52; R. J. Overy, *Why the Allies Won* (London: Cape, 1995); Thomas J. Christensen, *Useful Adversaries: Grand Strategy, Domestic Mobilization, and Sino-American Conflict, 1947–58* (Princeton: Princeton University Press, 1996); John J. Mearsheimer, *Liddell Hart and the Weight of History* (Ithaca: Cornell University Press, 1988); and Donald Kagan, *The Outbreak of the Peloponnesian War* (Ithaca: Cornell University Press, 1969), chap. 19, "The Causes of the War," pp. 345–56.

8. Examples of historical evaluative works include Bruce M. Russett, *No Clear and Present Danger: A Skeptical View of the U.S. Entry into World War II* (New York: Harper & Row, 1972); John Mueller, "Pearl Harbor: Military Inconvenience, Political Disaster," *International Security* 16 (Winter 1991–92): 172–203; Paul M. Kennedy, "Tirpitz, England and the Second Navy Law of 1900: A Strategical Critique," *Militaergeschichtliche Mitteilungen* 2 (1970): 33–57; Paul Kennedy, *Strategy and Diplomacy, 1870–1945* (Aylesbury, U.K.: Fontana, 1983), chap. 5, "Strategic Aspects of the Anglo-German Naval Race," and chap. 7, "Japanese Strategic Decisions, 1939–1945"; Gerhard Ritter, *The Schlieffen Plan: Critique of a Myth,* trans. Andrew Wilson and Eva Wilson, foreword by B. H. Liddell Hart (London: Oswald Wolff, 1958; reprint, Westport, Conn.: Greenwood Press, 1979); Robert W. Tucker and David C. Hendrickson, *The Imperial Temptation: The New World Order and America's Purpose* (New York: Council on Foreign Relations, 1992), part 2, "The Gulf War: An Autopsy"; Alan T. Nolan, *Lee Considered: General Robert E. Lee and Civil War History* (Chapel Hill: University of North Carolina Press, 1991); and Paul W. Schroeder, *The Axis Alliance and Japanese-American Relations, 1941* (Ithaca: Cornell University Press, 1958), chap. 9, "An Appraisal of American Policy," pp. 200–216.

then what are they for? Theories have value only if they are eventually put to work to explain, assess, or prescribe.

Moreover, scholarship of types 5 and 6 lacks a friendly home in other disciplines, which leaves this work to political scientists. Some historians are averse to explicit explanation, instead preferring to "let the facts speak for themselves." Others will elaborate a preferred explanation, but they rarely set contending explanations against one another, as one must to fully evaluate an explanation. Historians are also (with some exceptions)[9] generally averse to writing evaluative history. However, without explanatory historical work history is never explained; and without evaluative historical work we learn little from the past about present and future problem-solving. Hence some field should accept these tasks. I nominate political science.

7. A *predictive* dissertation applies theories to extrapolate the future world from current events or from posited future developments.[10] A purely predictive dissertation is a risky project because the future is constantly happening, raising the danger that the project may be overtaken by events. Therefore, students should generally steer clear of dissertations of this sort. However, this warning isn't iron-clad. Predictive work can be valuable and can take dissertation form.

These seven types of dissertation can be summarized as falling into four categories: theory-proposing (1), theory-testing (2), theory-applying (4, 5, 6, and 7), and literature-assessing (3). Dissertations of Type 1 and 2—theory-making and theory-

9. See, for instance, the works by Paul Kennedy, Gerhard Ritter, and Paul Schroeder cited in note 8.
10. Recent examples of predictive work include Robert Jervis, "The Future of World Politics: Will It Resemble the Past?" *International Security* 16 (Winter 1991–92): 39–73; John J. Mearsheimer, "Back to the Future: Instability in Europe after the Cold War," ibid., vol. 15 (Summer 1990): 5–56; and Stephen Van Evera, "Primed for Peace: Europe after the Cold War," ibid., 15 (Winter 1990–1991): 7–57. The latter two pieces also offer policy prescriptions, but their main thrust is predictive.

testing—have the most cachet in political science, but all seven types are legitimate if they are well done. Be clear in your own mind about which type of dissertation you are doing. Finally, some words on descriptive dissertations are in order. Such dissertations describe political circumstances.[11] They come in two types: contemporary descriptive (focusing on current developments and conditions)[12] and historical descriptive (focusing on past events and conditions).[13]

11. Description establishes data points: explanation explains the structure of data that has already been described. The following statements illustrate the difference: "In January 1991 oil sold for $40 per barrel on the world market" (pure description); and "In late 1990 the Persian Gulf crisis caused consumer fear that war might disrupt global oil supplies, which caused panic oil buying, which pushed up oil prices from under $20 to $40" (description and explanation—the price of oil is described and explained).

12. Examples of contemporary / descriptive work include articles from the 1980s describing the conventional military balance in central Europe: see John J. Mearsheimer, "Why the Soviets Can't Win Quickly in Central Europe," *International Security* 7 (Summer 1982): 3–39; John J. Mearsheimer, "Numbers, Strategy, and the European Balance," ibid., vol. 12 (Spring 1988): 174–85; Barry R. Posen, "Measuring the Conventional European Balance: Coping with Complexity in Threat Assessment," ibid., vol. 9 (Winter 1984–85): 47–88; and Barry R. Posen, "Is NATO Decisively Outnumbered?" ibid., vol. 12 (Spring 1988): 186–202. Note, however, that these works are not theory-barren. Both authors depend on causal hypotheses—e.g., the 3:1 rule and the force-to-space ratio hypothesis—hence their description is theory-reliant.

Examples on other topics include Steve Fetter, "Ballistic Missiles and Weapons of Mass Destruction: What Is the Threat? What Should Be Done?" *International Security* 16 (Summer 1991): 5–42; Bruce G. Blair, *Strategic Command and Control* (Washington, D.C.: Brookings, 1985); and Ashton B. Carter, "Assessing Command System Vulnerability," in Ashton B. Carter, John D. Steinbruner, and Charles A. Zraket, eds. *Managing Nuclear Operations* (Washington, D.C.: Brookings Institution, 1987), pp. 555–610. (These pieces are not purely descriptive; they also offer prescriptions, but their main focus is descriptive.)

13. Examples of works by political scientists that are largely historical / descriptive include Fred Kaplan, *The Wizards of Armageddon* (New York: Simon & Schuster, 1983); Scott Sagan, "Nuclear Alerts and Crisis Management," *International Security* 9 (Spring 1985): 99–139; and Richard K. Betts, *Soldiers, Statesmen, and Cold War Crises* (Cambridge: Harvard University Press, 1977). Such works by historians include John Lewis Gaddis, *Strategies of Containment: A Critical Appraisal of Postwar American National Security Policy* (New York: Oxford University Press, 1982); David Alan Rosenberg, "The Origins of Overkill: Nuclear Weapons

A descriptive dissertation is an eighth possible type of political science dissertation; however, a purely descriptive thesis will be poorly received by other political scientists. They want authors to explain or evaluate the events, policies, or ideas they describe. Hence description should be combined with some making, testing, or application of theory. Description must often precede explanation or evaluation, however, since phenomena that have not been described cannot be explained or evaluated. Hence students who seek to explain or evaluate phenomena that others have not fully described must first devote heavy attention to description, giving rise to largely descriptive dissertations. This is fine as long as the student also does some explaining or evaluation.[14]

---

and American Strategy, 1945–1960," *International Security* 7 (Spring 1983): 3–71; Luigi Albertini, *The Origins of the War of 1914*, 3 vols., trans. and ed. Isabella M. Massey (London: Oxford University Press, 1952–57; reprint, Westport, Conn.: Greenwood Press, 1980); and Holger Herwig, "Clio Deceived: Patriotic Self-Censorship in Germany After the Great War," *International Security* 12 (Fall 1987): 5–44. These works all provide some explanation, and several do some theory-testing, but their focus is descriptive.

14. A good dissertation of this kind is Peter J. Liberman, "Does Conquest Pay? The Exploitation of Occupied Industrial Economies" (Ph.D. diss., MIT, 1991); later published as *Does Conquest Pay? The Exploitation of Occupied Industrial Societies* (Princeton: Princeton University Press, 1996). Liberman devotes substantial space to description because previous scholarship left the phenomenon he explains (the benefits of empire) largely undescribed. He then develops and tests explanations for the patterns he describes.

Helpful Hints on
Writing a Political
Science Dissertation

I often make the following suggestions to graduate students who are launching dissertations.[1]

Topic Selection

A good dissertation asks an important question. The answer should be relevant to real problems facing the real world.

Hans Morgenthau once lamented that social scientists often hide in "the trivial, the formal, the methodological, the purely theoretical, the remotely historical—in short, the politically irrelevant."[2] Such conduct is both a crime and a blunder. Being relevant

1. A number of useful guidebooks on this topic have appeared in recent years. Especially valuable are David Madsen, *Successful Dissertations and Theses: A Guide to Graduate Student Research from Proposal to Completion*, 2d ed. (San Francisco: Jossey-Bass, 1992), and David Sternberg, *How to Complete and Survive a Doctoral Dissertation* (New York: St. Martin's Griffin, 1981). Also see my bibliography.

2. Hans J. Morgenthau, "The Purpose of Political Science," in James C. Charlesworth, ed., *A Design for Political Science: Scope, Objectives, and Methods* (Philadelphia: American Academy of Political and Social Science, 1966), p. 73.

is more fun, better for the world, and a good career move. Scholars who advance bold arguments win more praise than abuse if their work is sound. Research gains visibility largely by having college teachers assign it. Teachers assign work that frames debates. Hence work that boldly presents a side in an important debate or starts its own debate will be more widely assigned and thus more renowned. Its author will bask in academic fame and glory.

How can good topics be found? Starting yesterday, keep a "Books and Articles That Someone Should Write" file. When you form a mental picture of something you want to read, but a search reveals that it doesn't exist, record its hypothetical title and stash it in your "Books and Articles" file. Many of these absent articles won't be suitable projects for you, but some will. The rest are possible topics for your friends and future students. You do a major service by devising projects they can execute.

After each graduate school class, write an audit memo about the subject area of the course asking what was missing. What important questions went unasked? What answers did you expect to find in the literature that never appeared? What research projects could provide these answers?

Ph.D. qualifying exams offer another opportunity to audit the field for fillable holes. You have surveyed the field's horizon: now write a memo on questions and answers that turned up missing in the literature and research that could provide the missing answers.

Dissertation topics can also be found in public policy debates.

Morgenthau further complained of a "new scholasticism," in academe—the pursuit of "an intellectual exercise . . . that tells us nothing we need to know about the real world" (p. 74). Scholars maintain their reputations by "engaging in activities that can have no relevance for the political problems of the day"; instead they substitute a "fanatical devotion to esoteric terminology and mathematical formulas, equations and charts, in order to elucidate or obscure the obvious." As a result, social science resembles "a deaf man answering questions which no one has asked him." Hans J. Morgenthau, *Truth and Power* (New York: Praeger, 1970), pp. 246, 261.

First, read up on a policy debate you care about. Then identify the key disputes of fact or theory that drive opposing sides to their opposite conclusions. Then devise a research project that addresses one or more of these disputes.[3] This search method locates research questions that are unresolved and germane to important public policy questions.[4]

Organization

A good dissertation has a thesis—a main line of argument, or a set of related arguments.[5] If your dissertation lacks a thesis, think it through again. If your dissertation has too many theses, consider ways to organize your ideas more simply.

Your Dissertation Prospectus

Your dissertation prospectus supports your applications for research support money. Your prospectus should be five to ten pages long. It should frame the question(s) you will address, the reasons why these questions are worth exploring, your working hypotheses (the answers you expect to find), your methods of inquiry, and the reasons why you chose these methods.

You should footnote your prospectus as you would a research paper. Good bibliographic footnotes to existing work on your topic are important.

Before sending it out, circulate your prospectus among friends and colleagues for their comments and criticisms.[6]

3. Charles Glaser recommends this search method for research topics.
4. Also useful on topic selection are Madsen, *Successful Dissertations,* pp. 32–50, and Sternberg, *How to Complete and Survive a Doctoral Dissertation,* pp. 91–105.
5. Purely historical or descriptive theses are exempt from this requirement, but their authors should still identify and highlight any theme or structure that emerges in the material they present.
6. Also see Chapter 5 for more on the dissertation prospectus.

Your Introductory Chapter

The introduction and conclusion are the most-read parts of most dissertations and the only-read parts of many, hence their design merits special attention.

You should start your dissertation with a summary introduction chapter. A summary introduction helps readers measure your evidence against your claims and arguments by clarifying these claims and arguments at the outset. This makes your work more readable.

Your summary introduction should answer six (6) questions:

1. What question or questions do you address? Spell them out clearly. A dissertation can propose theories, test theories, explain historical events, or evaluate past or present policies or policy proposals. It can summarize and assess a body of literature. It can describe contemporary circumstances or historical events. It can do several or all of the above. State clearly which of these missions your dissertation fulfills.

Frame your questions in terms that call for specific answers. Questions that begin "how can we understand" ("How can we understand the meaning of the nuclear revolution?" or "How can we understand the process by which nationalism arises?") are so open-ended that vacuous nonresponses ("We can understand the meaning of the nuclear revolution by reading Bob Jervis") technically qualify as answers. Focused questions are better: "What are the consequences of the nuclear revolution?", or "What are the causes of nationalism?" Questions that inquire about "cause" or "consequence," or that pose specific descriptive tasks ("How numerous were Stalin's victims?") are better, since readers can more easily tell if you answer them.

2. Why do these questions arise—from what scholarly literature or real-world events? What previous literature has been written on these questions? What is the "state of the art" on the subject?

If your questions arise from an evolving scholarly literature, you should discuss that literature in the text of your introduction and note ancillary or related literature in footnotes. Note any controversies in this literature, explain their origins and evolution, detail the arguments made by both sides, and summarize their current status. Note the factual or theoretical crux of any continuing disagreements. Note also the holes in the current literature. What questions have *not* been explored? (Let's hope yours is among them.) You also might interpret the motives that sustain continuing controversies. What, if any, political or methodological motives are driving the disputants apart? Are these disputants honest scholars or paid polemicists? In short, explain what's been going on in the field you are entering.

If your questions arise from historical or contemporary events, detail these events, explain their significance, and explain why they give rise to the question or questions you address. Also mention any existing literature on the subject you address, and note holes in that literature.[7]

3. What answer or answers will you offer? *Clearly summarize your conclusions in your introduction.* Your summary should offer enough detail to let readers grasp the main elements of your argument by reading your introduction alone. It should run several pages at least.

The opposite strategy, of seducing readers by withholding conclusions until late in the document, merely tries readers' patience. Moreover, your argument is lost on the many readers who won't read past your introduction.

4. What competing explanations, arguments, interpretations, or frameworks will you reject or refute?[8] Clearly identify the books, articles, and ideas that you demolish.

Connect your dissertation to all the debates and literatures that

7. Regarding sequence, a gracefully written first chapter can start with your questions or with their historical / factual context. It can work better to first frame the facts that stir your questions, then frame the questions these facts inspire.
8. Graceful chapter construction may be served by addressing this question and question 2 at the same time.

it speaks to. If it speaks to several debates or literatures, flag this so participants in each debate will realize that your work matters to them. This helps them and also you: they will cite you and make you famous.

5. How will you reach your answers? Say a few words about your methodology and sources. If you are doing case studies, explain how you selected your cases. If you are doing archival research, say so, and identify the archives and sources you used. If you are doing interviews, offer some remarks on your interview subjects and procedures. If you are doing a large-n statistical study, explain the origins and construction of the data bases you are using, and explain your method of analysis—in terms comprehensible to the many among your readers who have forgotten their statistics. If you are using other evidence, for example, press accounts, explain its nature. If your approach is largely deductive, explain this.

If there are methods or sources that readers might expect you to use, but that for some reason you did not use, you might note this and explain your decisions. Evidence that proved to be unavailable and lines of research that proved infeasible might be mentioned. If there are important questions that you did not answer, identify these and explain why you could not answer them. Instead of writing your way around gaps in your research, explain them honestly in your introduction. (But do your research in a way that doesn't require lame excuses.)

6. What comes next? Provide a roadmap to the rest of the dissertation: "Chapter 1 explains how I began my life of crime; Chapter 2 details early arrests; Chapter 3 describes my road to death row; Chapter 4 offers general theoretical conclusions and policy implications." Something of that sort.

Subjects 1 ("What is your question?"), 2 ("Why does this question arise?"), and 3 ("What is your answer?") are the most important. Make sure you cover these with care.

Summary introductions of this sort reduce confusion about

what your dissertation does and does not say. They also serve a diagnostic purpose for the author. The act of drafting a summary can alert you to internal contradictions or other flaws in the structure of your argument. This helps you flag problems that need fixing.

Your introduction should be the first chapter you draft and the last chapter you finish. Since it summarizes your dissertation you can't complete it until the other chapters are done and you know what they say. So don't spend effort polishing it until the rest of your dissertation is written.

Your Concluding Chapter

In your conclusion you may want to summarize your questions and answers, if your summary introduction was cursory. However, I recommend that you recapitulate your research only briefly and then explore its implications at greater length. What policy implications follow from your discoveries? Which general theories does it call into question, and which does it reinforce? What broader historical questions does it raise or settle? What further research is called for by your discoveries? This is the place to discuss the larger significance of your research.

Study Design and Presentation: Observe Cumulative Knowledge Norms

Political science is often criticized because few questions are ever settled and the same issues are revisited over and over. Things will improve if social scientists follow practices that foster the accumulation of knowledge. So please follow these injunctions:

1. Have a research design before you start your research. This platitude is too often honored in the breach. "The main purpose of

the [research] design is to help to avoid the situation in which the evidence does not address the initial research questions."[9] Those who proceed without a research design risk being marooned on a mismatch between their questions and their evidence.

2. Frame your argument clearly. Knowledge accumulates only if your readers know what you have said.

If your dissertation proposes, tests, or applies theories, the reader should be able to "arrow-diagram" these theories.[10] If your hypotheses cannot be reduced to arrow diagrams, then your writing and probably your thinking are too muddy. Think your project through again. This advice applies to explicitly theoretical work and to policy-prescriptive work. All policy prescription rests on theories, and good prescriptive writing frames these theories clearly.

If your dissertation is largely descriptive or historical, your main discoveries should be clearly summarized at least once in the dissertation, preferably at the outset.

If your dissertation tests theories or explanations, clearly frame their predictions (or "observable implications") before presenting evidence. Theories and explanations are tested by inferring predictions from the explanation and then asking if the predictions are confirmed or disconfirmed by the evidence. You should explicate this process for your readers by clearly framing the predictions your evidence tests. (Most authors omit this step but that doesn't make it wise.)

Frame all predictions that flow from your theory, including those that are falsified by the evidence or prove untestable. Failed predictions should be identified and their failure confessed. If some predictions are confirmed and some fail, say so and offer interpretation.

Thus your overall format should be (a) frame your theory/

9. Robert K. Yin, *Case Study Research: Design and Methods*, 2d ed. (Thousand Oaks, Calif.: Sage, 1994), p. 20.
10. On arrow-diagrams see the section "What Is a Theory?" in Chapter 1.

explanation; (b) infer predictions from it; (c) perform tests; and (d) offer interpretation.

3. Be definitive. Your dissertation should reflect a comprehensive survey of literature and evidence relevant to your subject. Your footnotes should provide a comprehensive bibliography to the important literature relevant to your topic. This requires that you gain mastery of all aspects of your subject.

4. Document all sources and statements of fact. This requires a good personal system for storing and retrieving your evidence. One of my rules of thumb: when in doubt, make photocopies. Copy everything you might use or cite in your dissertation. This eases data retrieval and documentation of sources.

5. "Argue against yourself." Acknowledge counterarguments that might be raised by skeptical readers and briefly address them later in the text. Concede what you should to these arguments and explain why you won't concede more. This shows readers that you have given due thought to possible objections or alternate interpretations. It also forestalls baseless criticism of your work.

6. Do plausibility probes as the first phase of your research. In other words, find out the answer before doing your study. The experimental science model proceeds from question to hypothesis to prediction to experiment to conclusion. This mechanistic program seldom works for us. Instead we go from question to hypothesis to prediction to data exploration (plausibility probe) to revised hypothesis to prediction to larger data exploration to conclusion. In short, we often "work backward" from answer to proof.[11] We must do this to narrow the range of possible answers we fully investigate. Otherwise we would waste energy doing full-dress tests of hypotheses that a cursory look at the data would refute.

7. Clearly identify works that your dissertation revises, con-

---

11. Of course, if deeper study refutes the results of our plausibility probe we report this. Scholars go where the evidence takes them.

tradicts, or supersedes. If your dissertation is theoretical or policy-prescriptive, identify by name those authors whose works you refute. If your dissertation is descriptive or historical, identify exactly which previous accounts you are revising. This may annoy the superseded authors, but otherwise your readers will continue to quote outmoded work.

How can you sharpen your methodological skills? Reread works you admire, keeping an eye on how the authors executed their projects. Form an attitude on what they did right and wrong and note the methods and sources they used. Consider whether similar methods or sources might be appropriate for your possible dissertation project.

Writing

A well-written dissertation is more likely to be published, assigned, and quoted. So bear the following points in mind:

1. That which is simple is also good. Your dissertation should make a single main point or handful of related points. It should have a clear, simple structure.

Avoid cluttering your dissertation with extra ornaments and gargoyles (as students often do). Just because you researched something doesn't mean it belongs in the manuscript. Cutting is painful—"I sweated hours over this!"—too bad! In the world of research, half your work is done to be thrown away or saved for a later project.

The logic of presentation varies from the logic of discovery. Your research followed the logic of discovery, but your write-up should follow the logic of presentation. This means it should move simply and clearly from your questions to your answers. It is seldom wise to present your discoveries in the same order in which you made them.

Pitch your writing at a level appropriate for college under-graduate readers. Do not write at a level that only your faculty supervisors can understand. Scholarship that isn't used in the college classroom has little impact; hence you should take pains to address the average student.

2. The following structure is often appropriate for dissertation chapters:

a. Your argument;

b. Your supporting evidence;

c. Counterarguments, qualifications, and limiting conditions of your argument;

d. Brief concluding remarks, which may include comments on the implications of your argument, or may note questions they raise.

3. Start each chapter with several paragraphs summarizing the argument presented in the chapter. You may cut these summaries from your final draft if they seem redundant with your summary introduction but include them in your first drafts. They will help your supervisor and friends to read and comment on individual chapters. You may also want to keep these summaries in if they seem to fit. Finally, forcing yourself to summarize your argument in each chapter is a good way to make yourself confront contradictions or shortcomings in that argument.

Often these chapter summaries are best written after you write the chapter but don't forget to add them at some point.

4. Start each paragraph with a topic sentence that distills the point of the paragraph.[12] Later sentences should offer supporting material that explains or elaborates the point of the topic sentence. Qualifications or refutation to counterarguments should then follow. In short, paragraphs should have the same structure as whole chapters.

---

12. The topic sentence can appear as the second sentence in a paragraph but should not appear later than that.

A reader should be able to grasp the thrust of your dissertation by reading only the first couple of sentences of every paragraph.

5. Break chapters into numbered sections and subsections. More subsections are better than fewer; they help your readers follow your argument. Label each section or subsection with a vivid section heading that communicates the meaning of the section.

6. Write short, declarative sentences. Avoid the passive voice. (Passive voice: "The kulaks were murdered"—but who did it? Active voice: "Stalin murdered the kulaks.")

For more advice on writing see William Strunk Jr. and E. B. White, *The Elements of Style,* 3d ed. (New York: Macmillan, 1979), and Teresa Pelton Johnson, "Writing for *International Security:* A Contributor's Guide," *International Security* 16 (Fall 1991): 171–80.[13]

7. If you are doing case studies: it often works to write detailed chronological histories of the case before doing the case study. This helps you gain mastery of the case. Then reorganize your material into a case study.

Style

Acquire the manual on style (citation format, bibliography format, and so on) recommended by your department or university before you start your research, and check the sections on documentation and bibliography. This insures you will collect all appropriate citation information as you do your research. Otherwise you may have to waste time later retracing your steps to collect the required information.

Three general style formats are common: (1) the University of

13. Other useful guides to writing are listed in my bibliography.

Chicago format, which puts references to sources in footnotes or endnotes; (2) the Modern Language Association (MLA) format, which incorporates references parenthetically within the text; and (3) the American Psychological Association (APA) format, which also puts references parenthetically in the text but varies in other ways from the MLA format. The Chicago format is the most reader-friendly; the others clutter the text with references. Use Chicago if your department allows it.

The Chicago style rules are distilled in Kate L. Turabian, *A Manual for Writers of Term Papers, Theses, and Dissertations*, 6th ed., rev. John Grossman and Alice Bennett (Chicago: University of Chicago Press, 1996). Slavishly obey her instructions. Style mistakes make your manuscript look unprofessional.[14]

Vetting

When you finish some dissertation chapters, circulate them to several friends for comments and criticism. Don't be shy. The first law of scholarship is "two heads are better than one." Vetting will improve your work.

If your chapters are really half-baked—and early dissertation chapters usually are quite terrible—do show some caution. It is probably best not to show them to complete strangers, who may conclude from them that you are brain-dead, and that your respirator should be turned off. Do, however, show them to friends who can be trusted to know that you are not brain-dead, even

---

14. MLA style is presented in Joseph Garibaldi, *MLA Handbook for Writers of Research Papers*, 4th ed. (New York: Modern Language Association, 1995). APA style is presented in American Psychological Association, *Publication Manual of the American Psychological Association*, 4th ed. (Washington, D.C.: APA, 1994). All three styles—Chicago, MLA, and APA—are summarized in Carole Slade, William Giles Campbell, and Stephen Vaughan Ballou, *Form and Style: Research Papers, Reports, Theses*, 9th ed. (Boston: Houghton Mifflin, 1994).

though the condition of your chapters suggests otherwise, and who will help you kick them into shape.

Conversely, when others ask you to vet their work, you should take the task seriously. Helping others improve their written work is an important professional obligation. In carrying out this obligation, show mercy and compassion if your colleague's work indicates early brain death—while also making clear that there is significant room for improvement, and offering specific feasible suggestions.

Do not look solely to your professors for vetting or criticism. Your friends should play an equal, perhaps even larger, role.

Graduate students sometimes view their fellow students as competitors to be kept at a distance and left unhelped. This is a serious error, for two reasons. First, it is not menschlike. You should axiomatically, in your personal and professional life, aspire to be a mensch.[15] The world needs more mensches: so be one. Your mother and I both hope that you take this appeal to heart. We will be proud of you if you do. And mensches help their fellow students and colleagues. Second, aloofness from your fellow students is a career-management blunder. The history of social science lies in the record of triumphs and discoveries by scholars who formed empowering communities of mutual help and thereby outperformed their atomized colleagues. Those who act like piranhas often sink to the bottom, while those who help one another excel and prosper. Yes, Virginia, there is no conflict between collegial conduct and the imperatives of professional success. (On this matter study carefully Robert Axelrod's *Evolution of Cooperation*, pp. 63–66,[16] which summarizes the keys to success in academic life.)

---

15. Mensch: "an upright, honorable, decent person"; also "someone of consequence; someone to admire and emulate; someone of noble character" (from Yiddish). Leo Rosten, *The Joys of Yiddish* (New York: McGraw-Hill, 1968), p. 234. Mensch is an ungendered term that includes both sexes.

16. Robert Axelrod, *The Evolution of Cooperation* (New York: Basic Books, 1984).

Your Abstract

At an early stage, write a one- or two-page abstract that provides a clear, cogent summary of your dissertation. Circulate this abstract when you circulate draft chapters to help your readers grasp the general drift of what you are doing.

You should also include a provisional table of contents with chapter titles when you circulate draft chapters. This helps your readers see the big picture.[17]

Dealing with Your Dissertation Committee

Your adviser owes you a thoughtful reaction to your dissertation proposal and some reaction as you produce chapters. However, this is your dissertation not your adviser's. Your name goes on the cover. If you are really stuck—as you will be from time to time—ask for help, but don't expect anyone to hold your hand through the whole process. Your adviser has the right to expect you to solve most of your problems yourself and to seek your own solutions before asking others to get involved.

Your committee members owe you one but only one careful reading of your dissertation chapters. Do not expect iterated readings. A loving adviser may give you more than one but don't expect it. Hence you should carefully choose when you want your committee members to read your drafts.

Edit chapter drafts before showing them to your committee. It takes your committee far longer to read very rough drafts, and they are less able to make useful comments. So neaten everything up before sending it around. (If you want early mid-course correction from your committee, ask your adviser to react to a detailed outline not a half-baked draft.)

17. You might also include your prospectus when you circulate chapters to readers unfamiliar with your project, so they can grasp what you originally set out to do.

Listen carefully to your adviser's advice. Most of this advice will probably be wise, some will be misguided. You needn't follow the errant advice, but do have reasons for spurning advice you reject.

Do not make your adviser repeat things twice. Remember that when you deal with your adviser your professionalism is on display.

Dealing with Your Head, Your Family, and Your Friends

Writing a dissertation is a difficult and lonely act that requires great force of will. The best way to summon up this will is to choose a topic that fires you up. This consideration argues for choosing a topic that stirs your passions over topics that fit current field fashions but excite you less.

The spouses, significant others, parents, and friends of academics often fail to fully grasp the central importance and great difficulty of writing a dissertation. They grow impatient with the many months of strange behavior—the falling-down-manhole absentmindedness, the vacant stare, the seemingly permanent hermit-like disappearance into murky library stacks, the vast cluttering of the apartment with clouds of note cards and paper, mumbling to yourself when others can hear you, and so on. You must be strong against these enemies of knowledge. Forgive them for their ignorance and abuse but do not concede to their entreaties to goof off on weekends, go to the beach, have a beer, or otherwise act like a normal person. Those who have not written dissertations can never understand how important it is to remain focused on the project. The best you can do is explain to them, over and over, that your career rides on writing a decent dissertation, and that writing a decent dissertation is like climbing Mount Everest: it can be done, but only by careful preparation and intense focus on the task. If this doesn't work, take solace in the fellowship of dissertation-writing friends who are in the same fix and hope the divorce papers don't arrive before you get your degree.

How to Learn More about How to Write a Dissertation

Reread several books you like that used approaches similar to yours and imitate their better aspects.[18]

18. For example, I recommend that students doing historical case studies look at Barry Posen, *Sources of Military Doctrine* (Ithaca: Cornell University Press, 1984), and Stephen Walt, *Origins of Alliances* (Ithaca: Cornell University Press, 1987). The theory chapters of these books are well done; when in doubt, imitate them when doing your own theory chapter.

The Dissertation Proposal

Your dissertation proposal explains your project to the world. You will use it to persuade funders and research institutions to support you and to elicit comments and suggestions on your project from friends and colleagues.

It should frame the question(s) your dissertation will answer and explain how you propose to answer them. It also should persuade readers that your questions are important, and your plan of action is practical.[1]

A proposal should answer five questions:

1. What question or questions do you address?

2. Why does this question arise? (From what scholarly debates or real-world events?) Why does it matter? Say a few words about the origins and significance of your project.

3. What previous literature has been written on the question? Describe the "state of the art" on the subject.

---

1. Other useful discussions of proposal-writing include David Madsen, *Successful Dissertations and Theses: A Guide to Graduate Student Research from Proposal to Completion,* 2d ed. (San Francisco: Jossey-Bass, 1992), pp. 51–80; David Sternberg, *How to Complete and Survive a Doctoral Dissertation* (New York: St. Martin's Griffin, 1981), pp. 72–107.

If a substantial literature has already appeared on the subject you address, you should explain and distinguish majority and minority views (providing footnotes to relevant literature), and sketch the manner in which important relevant controversies have evolved.

Note: Questions 2 and 3 overlap and can often be answered together in a single statement.

4. What working hypotheses will you explore? You can't be sure of your answer until you complete your research, but readers want to know what hunches you plan to investigate.

5. How will you reach your answers? Say a few words about the methodology you are choosing, why you are choosing it, and how you will implement it. If you are doing case studies, identify your cases and explain their selection. If you are analyzing large-n data bases, identify and describe them. If you are doing interviews or other field research, briefly explain how you plan to go about it. If you are doing survey research, briefly describe your survey sources. If you are doing archival research, explain which archives and sources you will use. If you are using other records, e.g., press accounts, make this clear. If your approach is largely deductive, explain this. If there are methods that readers might expect you to use, but that for some reason you will not use, you might note this and briefly explain your decisions.

You should answer these questions in roughly five to ten typed double-spaced pages. Footnote your proposal as you would a research paper. It may also be appropriate to append a preliminary bibliography of one to two pages listing some of the sources that you plan to consult.

To learn more about how to write a proposal, ask a friend who has written a reputedly good proposal if you can look at what they did. Pay close heed to proposals that were well received by others.

CHAPTER 6

Professional Ethics

Many professions have codes of ethics and teach professional ethics in their professional schools. For example, most students of law, business, and medicine now take a course in professional ethics at some point.

The social sciences should also discuss and teach professional ethics, for three reasons. First, the wider world cannot easily hold us accountable for our general professional performance. No market forces compel us to deliver a useful research product. Absent this pressure we risk degenerating into social parasites. (Groups that are accountable to none seldom serve any well and often turn parasitic or worse.) A shared body of professional ethics that defines our obligations to society can reduce the accountability gap by helping us to hold our own feet to the fire.

Second, our students cannot easily hold us accountable. If we teach badly, there is little they can do about it. Hence we must hold ourselves accountable to perform as teachers. A body of ethics that defines our teaching obligations can be a self-accountability mechanism.

Third, the lack of shared norms among ourselves on proper conduct in all manner of personal and professional settings causes confusion and even tragedies that injure involved parties and consume the time of others who must act as judges. These confusions and tragedies could be reduced by reaching a wider and clearer agreement on professional norms of conduct toward each other.

Issues to cover in a course module on professional ethics might include:

1. What do social scientists owe the outside world? Relevance? Honesty? Anything? Do we have a social contract of some sort with wider society, or are we free to conduct ourselves however we please?

One view is that social science has a duty to be relevant. We have an implicit contract with society: in exchange for academic freedoms and privileges we agree to spend at least some energy answering society's more urgent questions. This does not require headline chasing. We can meet our obligation with policy research or with more abstract work that could have policy implications far down the road. But social science violates its contract if it drifts into complete irrelevance, as much of it has.

Social science also has a duty to be unpopular if necessary. Many important social ideas have distributive effects that injure someone—often someone who is noisy or powerful. Taking their heat is part of our job. We should expect it and remain undiverted by it. We are given the privilege of tenure in part so we can stand up to it, and we waste and abuse that privilege if we let fear of criticism divert our work.

Intellectual fashion-surfing and middle-straddling should be discouraged when they replace the speaking of unwelcome truths.

2. What do social scientists owe their students?

One view is that a teacher's mission is to produce learned men and women who think great thoughts of their own. This requires curbing our urge to clone ourselves and giving our students full latitude to form their own ideas, including (horrors) ideas that clash with ours.

We all love our own ideas, but the place to frame them is in our written work. There we should argue a clear point of view. In our teaching we should pose puzzles and present both sides. Students should be asked to come up with their own answers. In short, teachers should bifurcate their work: arguing their ideas in their writings; teaching others how to think (hence imposing few answers) in their teaching.

Teachers also owe the teaching of skills that are little fun to teach, for example, writing. Teaching writing is an important duty of college teachers. Most of us would rather talk about substance than about writing but teaching it is part of our job.

3. What do social scientists owe each other? Impartiality in reviewing manuscripts, fellowship applications, tenure review? Civility of discourse? Generosity in sharing of ideas? General menschlike conduct?

One view is that diversity of methods and arguments should be maintained. A diverse marketplace of ideas and methods produces the best results.

In hiring we are entitled, indeed obliged, to define the boundaries of social science and to exclude that which lies beyond it. Tolerance does not require that we hire and tenure witch doctors and alchemists. But subfield hegemonism should be frowned upon. Scholars badly serve their department, students, and field by reflexively trying to clone their method or topical subfield to the point of exterminating others.

In reviewing manuscripts we should exclude agreement or disagreement with an author's argument as criteria to recommend for or against publication. Reviewers should endorse manuscripts that ably and seriously make important arguments, even if the argument sets the reviewer's teeth on edge. We learn through debate. Debate requires that diverse views get a hearing in print. Reviewers should render judgments that foster this diversity.

Conversely, mutual backscratching in reviewing is a form of corruption. Do not cut your personal friends and methodological or ideological soulmates any breaks when reviewing manuscripts. Corrupt backscratching occurs in our field but that does not make it right.

Civility of discourse must be preserved. We should state arguments forcefully but ad hominem attack should be kept to a minimum. Arguments should stick to the logic and the evidence of the case and should be so judged. Otherwise discourse degrades into personal wars from which the community learns little.

Scholars should staunchly defend all other scholars' academic freedom of speech. We have a duty to protect our bitterest opponent's right to be heard. Civil discourse collapses if we fail to do this (an important lesson of the 1960s).

The assemblers of data and the inventors of ideas deserve first crack at their use, but scholarship is most productive when scholars share with each other. Data-hogging, document-hogging, and even idea-hogging are doubtful practices.

Mensches make the world go round, and this should be recognized in funding, hiring and promotion decisions. The success of an academic field depends in part on whether it has at least some fair-minded, public-spirited people among its leaders. Such individuals set a moral tone for the field, act as fair brokers to resolve disputes, serve as good examples for younger scholars, and reassure these younger scholars that the field will be run in a meritocratic fashion. Without such leaders academic fields are bound to degenerate into intellectual corruption and internecine conflict. Hence some value should be placed on menschhood in personnel decisions.

4. Love, romance, etc.

A sound general rule is: no romance of any kind across power lines. Faculty and graduate students are adults, and adult human beings do mate with each other, often with others who share their intellectual interests. However, romance across power lines, that is, between two people one of whom has power over the other, should be strictly taboo. When such romance seems a good idea to both parties, the power relationship should be clearly and permanently ended before romancing begins. The more powerful party should formally recuse him- or herself from all further decision making regarding the less powerful party. If this is for some reason administratively impossible (as it often will be), then romance is a very poor idea: it may be sexual harassment in the eyes of the weaker party, and it will be generally corrupting to the professional integrity of both parties.

Even if the stronger party can recuse him- or herself, he or she still cannot properly initiate romance because the suggestion of romance by the stronger is coercive by its nature: the weaker party may fear that rejecting the stronger will lead to retaliation. Hence stronger parties with romantic thoughts must keep these to themselves unless the weaker raises the subject.

How to Write a Paper

I often offer the following suggestions to undergraduates writing class papers.

General Format

The following general format is often appropriate: "tell them what you're going to tell them; then tell them; then tell them what you told them."

Introduction Format

Begin your paper with a short summary introduction. This summary introduction should answer up to five (5) questions:

1. What question or questions do you address?

2. Why do these questions arise? From what literature or real-world events? Offer background that clarifies your questions and puts them in context.

3. What answer or answers do you offer? Summarize your bottom line in a few sentences.

4. How will you reach your answers? Say a few words about your sources and methods.

5. What comes next? Provide a roadmap to the rest of the paper: "Section I explains how I began my life of crime; Section II details my early arrests; Section III describes my trip to death row; Section IV offers general theoretical conclusions and policy implications." Something of that sort.

Number 1 ("What is your question?"), number 2 ("Why does this question arise?"), and number 3 ("What is your answer?") are essential: make sure you cover them. Numbers 4 and 5 are optional.

Summary introductions of this sort help readers grasp your argument. They also help you diagnose problems with your paper. A summary introduction can be hard to write. A possible reason: gaps or contradictions in your arguments or evidence, which summary exposes. Solution: rethink and reorganize your paper.

Conclusion Format

Authors often recapitulate their argument in their conclusion; however, a good summary introduction often makes a full summary conclusion redundant. If so, recapitulate quickly and then use your conclusion to explore the implications of your argument. What policy prescriptions follow from your analysis? What general arguments does it call into question, and which does it reinforce? What further research projects does it suggest?

Argumentation

Four injunctions on argumentation should be kept in mind.

1. Use empirical evidence—facts, numbers, history—to support your argument. Purely deductive argument is sometimes

appropriate, but argument backed by evidence is always more persuasive.

2. Clearly frame the general point(s) that your evidence supports. Don't ask facts to speak for themselves.

To summarize points 1 and 2: offer evidence to support your arguments and state the arguments your evidence supports.

3. "Argue against yourself." After laying out your argument, acknowledge questions or objections that a skeptical reader might raise, and briefly address them. This shows readers that you were thoughtful, thorough, and paid due regard to possible objections or alternate interpretations.

Often, of course, the skeptic would have a good point, and you should grant it. Don't claim too much for your theories or evidence!

4. Use footnotes to document all sources and statements of fact. On footnote and citation format, consult and obey Kate L. Turabian, *A Manual for Writers of Term Papers, Theses, and Dissertations*, 6th ed., rev. John Grossman and Alice Bennett (Chicago: University of Chicago Press, 1996), in paperback. You should own a copy.

Writing

Good writing is essential to clear thinking and effective communication. So bear the following points in mind:

1. Your paper should make a single point or a handful of related points and should follow a simple organization. Avoid cluttering it with extra points. If you developed an argument that later became ancillary as you rethought your paper, drop the argument from the paper. This is painful ("I sweated hours on that idea!") but extraneous arguments drain power from your main argument.

2. Break your paper into numbered sections and subsections.

More sections is better than fewer. Sections help readers see the structure of your argument.

Label sections with vivid section headings that convey the main message of the section.

3. I recommend the following structure for sections/ subsections:

a. Your argument;

b. Your supporting evidence;

c. Counterarguments, qualifications, and limiting conditions of your argument.

4. Start each section with several sentences summarizing the argument presented in the section. You may cut these summaries from your final draft if they seem redundant with your summary introduction, but you should include them in your first drafts to see how they look. Writing such summaries is also a good way to force yourself to decide what you are and are not doing in each section, and to force yourself to confront contradictions or short-comings in your argument.

Often these section summaries are best written after you write the section, but don't forget to add them at some point.

5. Start each paragraph with a topic sentence that distills the point of the paragraph.[1] Later sentences should offer supporting material that explains or elaborates the point of the topic sentence. Qualifications or refutation to counterarguments should then follow. In short, paragraphs should have the same structure as whole sections.

A reader should be able to grasp the thrust of your argument by reading only the first couple of sentences of every paragraph.

6. Write short, declarative sentences. Avoid the passive voice. (Passive voice: "The kulaks were murdered"—but who did it? Active voice: "Stalin murdered the kulaks.")

---

1. The topic sentence can appear as the second sentence in a paragraph, but should not appear later than that.

7. Write from an outline. Outlines are major aids to coherence and readability.

8. Write at a level appropriate for college undergraduate readers—i.e., smart readers without much background knowledge on your topic. In fact your class papers will be read by teachers who probably know something about your topic, but they want to see how you would lay out your argument for folks who don't.

For more advice on writing see William Strunk Jr. and E. B. White, *The Elements of Style*, 3d ed. (New York: Macmillan, 1979), and Teresa Pelton Johnson, "Writing for International Security: A Contributor's Guide," *International Security* 16 (Fall 1991): 171–80.[2]

If you are doing a research paper, you might also consult Kate L. Turabian, *A Student's Guide to Writing College Papers*, 3d ed. (Chicago: University of Chicago Press, 1976), for advice.[3]

Vetting

Ask a friend or two to give your paper a look before you turn it in; and return the favor for them when they have a paper under

2. Other useful guides to writing include Claire Kehrwald Cook, *Line by Line: How to Edit Your Own Writing* (Boston: Houghton Mifflin, 1985); Frederick Crews, *The Random House Handbook*, 4th ed. (New York: Random House, 1984); Thomas S. Kane, *The New Oxford Guide to Writing* (New York: Oxford University Press, 1988).

3. Other primers include Roberta H. Markman, Peter T. Markman, and Marie L. Waddell, *10 Steps in Writing the Research Paper*, 5th ed. (New York: Barron's, 1989); Michael Meyer, *The Little, Brown Guide to Writing Research Papers* (Boston: Little, Brown, 1982); Audrey Roth, *The Research Paper: Process, Form, and Content*, 7th ed. (Belmont, Calif.: Wadsworth, 1995); Ellen Strenski and Madge Manfred, *The Research Paper Workbook*, 3d ed. (New York: Longman, 1992); Harry Teitelbaum, *How to Write a Thesis: A Guide to the Research Paper*, 3d ed. (New York: Macmillan, 1994); Stephen Weidenborner and Domenick Caruso, *Writing Research Papers: A Guide to the Process*, 5th ed. (New York: St. Martin's Press, 1997).

way. Two heads are better than one, and giving and receiving comments are important skills.

General Beauty Tips

Take care to turn in a neat, clean paper. Run your spellchecker. A messy-looking paper suggests a messy mind.

How to Learn More about How to Write Papers

Reread articles you or others admire and imitate their better aspects.

Further Reading

On the Case Study Method

Achen, Christopher H., and Duncan Snidal. "Rational Deterrence Theory and Comparative Case Studies." *World Politics* 41 (January 1989): 143–69.

Campbell, Donald T. "'Degrees of Freedom' and the Case Study." In Campbell, *Methodology and Epistemology for Social Science: Selected Papers*, pp. 377–88. Chicago: University of Chicago Press, 1988, first pub. 1974.

Collier, David. "The Comparative Method." In Ada W. Finifter, ed., *Political Science: The State of the Discipline*, 2d ed., pp. 105–20. Washington, D.C.: American Political Science Association, 1993.

Collier, David, and James Mahoney. "Insights and Pitfalls: Selection Bias in Qualitative Research." *World Politics* 49 (October 1996): 56–91.

Eckstein, Harry. "Case Study and Theory in Political Science." In Fred I. Greenstein and Nelson W. Polsby, eds., *Handbook of Political Science*, vol. 7, *Strategies of Inquiry*, pp. 79–137. Reading, Mass.: Addison-Wesley, 1975.

Geddes, Barbara. "How the Cases You Choose Affect the Answers You Get: Selection Bias in Comparative Cases." *Political Analysis* 2 (1990): 131–50.

George, Alexander L. "Case Studies and Theory Development: The Method of Structured, Focused Comparison." In Paul Gordon Lauren, ed., *Diplomacy: New Approaches in History, Theory, and Policy*, pp. 43–68. New York: Free Press, 1979.

——. "Case Studies and Theory Development." Paper presented to the Second Annual Symposium on Information Processing in Organizations, Carnegie-Mellon University, Pittsburgh, Pa., October 15–16, 1982.

——. "The Causal Nexus between Cognitive Beliefs and Decision-Making

Behavior: The 'Operational Code' Belief System." In Lawrence S. Falkowski, ed., *Psychological Models in International Politics*, pp. 95–124. Boulder, Colo.: Westview, 1979.

George, Alexander L., and Timothy J. McKeown. "Case Studies and Theories of Organizational Decision Making." In *Advances in Information Processing in Organizations*, 2:21–58. Greenwich, Conn.: JAI Press, 1985.

Hamel, Jacques, with Stéphane Dufour and Dominic Fortin. *Case Study Methods*, pp. 18–28. Newbury Park, Calif.: Sage, 1993.

King, Gary, Robert O. Keohane, and Sidney Verba. *Designing Social Inquiry: Scientific Inference in Qualitative Research*. Princeton: Princeton University Press, 1994.

Lieberson, Stanley. "Small N's and Big Conclusions: An Examination of the Reasoning in Comparative Studies Based on a Small Number of Cases." *Social Forces* 70 (December 1991): 307–20.

Lijphart, Arend. "The Comparable-Cases Strategy in Comparative Research." *Comparative Political Studies* 8 (July 1975): 158–77.

——. "Comparative Politics and the Comparative Method." *American Political Science Review* 65 (September 1971): 682–93.

Mill, John Stuart. "Of the Four Methods of Experimental Inquiry." Chapter 8 in *A System of Logic*, ed. J. M. Robson, pp. 388–406. Toronto: University of Toronto Press, 1973.

Platt, Jennifer. "'Case Study' in American Methodological Thought." *Current Sociology* 40 (Spring 1992): 42–43.

Przeworski, Adam. "Methods of Cross-National Research, 1970–83: An Overview." In Meinolf Dierkes, Hans N. Weiler, and Ariane Berthoin Antal, eds., *Comparative Policy Research: Learning from Experience*, pp. 31–49. Aldershot, England: Gower, 1987.

Przeworski, Adam, and Henry Teune. *The Logic of Comparative Social Inquiry*. Malabar, Fla.: Krieger, 1982.

Ragin, Charles C. *The Comparative Method: Moving Beyond Qualitative and Quantitative Strategies*. Berkeley: University of California Press, 1987.

Ragin, Charles C., and Howard S. Becker, eds. *What Is a Case? Exploring the Foundations of Social Inquiry*. Cambridge: Cambridge University Press, 1992.

Rogowski, Ronald. "The Role of Scientific Theory and Anomaly in Social-Scientific Inference." *American Political Science Review* 89 (June 1995): 467–70.

Skocpol, Theda. "Emerging Agendas and Recurrent Strategies in Historical Sociology." In Theda Skocpol, ed., *Vision and Method in Historical Sociology*, pp. 356–91. Cambridge: Cambridge University Press, 1984.

Skocpol, Theda, and Margaret Somers. "The Uses of Comparative History in Macrosocial Inquiry." *Comparative Studies in Society and History* 22 (April 1980): 174–97.

Smelser, Neil J. "The Methodology of Comparative Analysis." In Donald P. Warwick and Samuel Osherson, eds., *Comparative Research Methods*, pp. 42–86. Englewood Cliffs, N.J.: Prentice-Hall, 1973.

Stake, Robert E. "Case Studies." In Norman K. Denzin and Yvonna S. Lincoln, eds., *Handbook of Qualitative Research*, pp. 236–47. Thousand Oaks, Calif.: Sage, 1994.

Stoeker, Randy. "Evaluating and Rethinking the Case Study." *Sociological Review* 39 (February 1991): 88–112.

Yin, Robert K. *Case Study Research: Design and Methods.* 2d ed. Thousand Oaks, Calif.: Sage, 1994.

On Dissertation Writing

Becker, Howard S. With a chapter by Pamela Richards. *Writing for Social Scientists: How to Start and Finish Your Thesis, Book, or Article.* Chicago: University of Chicago Press, 1986.

Booth, Wayne C., Gregory G. Colomb, and Joseph M. Williams. *The Craft of Research.* Chicago: University of Chicago Press, 1995.

Hall, Peter A. "Helpful Hints for Writing Dissertations in Comparative Politics." *PS: Political Science and Politics* (December 1990): 596–98.

Krathwohl, David R. *How to Prepare a Research Proposal: Guidelines for Funding and Dissertations in the Social and Behavioral Sciences.* 3d ed. Syracuse: Syracuse University Press, 1988.

Madsen, David. *Successful Dissertations and Theses: A Guide to Graduate Student Research from Proposal to Completion.* 2d ed. San Francisco: Jossey-Bass, 1992.

Mauch, James E., and Jack W. Birch. *Guide to the Successful Thesis and Dissertation: Conception to Publication: A Handbook for Students and Faculty.* 3d ed. New York: M. Dekker, 1993.

Meloy, Judith M. *Writing the Qualitative Dissertation: Understanding by Doing.* Hillsdale, N.J.: Lawrence Erlbaum, 1994.

Miller, Joan I., and Bruce J. Taylor, *The Thesis Writer's Handbook: A Complete One-Source Guide for Writers of Research Papers.* West Linn, Oregon: Alcove, 1987.

Rudestam, Kjell, Erik Newton, and Rae R. Newton. *Surviving Your Dissertation: A Comprehensive Guide to Content and Process.* Newbury Park, Calif.: Sage, 1992.

Sternberg, David. *How to Complete and Survive a Doctoral Dissertation.* New York: St. Martin's Griffin, 1981.

Watson, George. *Writing a Thesis: A Guide to Long Essays and Dissertations.* New York: Longman, 1987.

On Academic Survival

Cryer, Pat. *The Research Student's Guide to Success.* Philadelphia: Open University Press, 1996.

DeNeef, A. Leigh, and Craufurd D. Goodwin, eds. *The Academic's Handbook,* 2d ed. Durham: Duke University Press, 1995.

Phillips, Estelle M., and D. S. Pugh. *How to Get a Ph.D.: Managing the Peaks and Troughs of Research.* Philadelphia: Open University Press, 1987.

Rossman, Mark H. *Negotiating Graduate School: A Guide for Graduate Students* Thousand Oaks, Calif.: Sage, 1995.

On Writing

Baker, Sheridan. *The Practical Stylist.* 5th ed. New York: HarperCollins, 1981.

Cook, Claire Kehrwald. *Line by Line: How to Edit Your Own Writing.* Boston: Houghton Mifflin, 1985.

Crews, Frederick. *The Random House Handbook.* 4th ed. New York: Random House, 1984.

Gowers, Ernest. *The Complete Plain Words.* 3d ed., rev. Sidney Greenbaum and Janet Whitcut. London: Her Majesty's Stationery Office, 1986.

Hacker, Diana. *Rules for Writers: A Brief Handbook.* 3d ed. Boston: St. Martin's, 1996.

Johnson, Teresa Pelton. "Writing for *International Security:* A Contributor's Guide." *International Security* 16 (Fall 1991): 171–80.

Kane, Thomas S. *The New Oxford Guide to Writing.* New York: Oxford University Press, 1988.

McCrimmon, James M., with Susan Miller and Webb Salmon. *Writing with a Purpose.* 9th ed. Boston: Houghton Mifflin, 1988.

Perrin, Porter G. *Writer's Guide and Index to English.* 5th ed. Glenview, Ill.: Scott, Foresman, 1972.

Strunk, William, Jr., and E. B. White. *The Elements of Style.* 3d ed. New York: Macmillan, 1979.

Williams, Joseph M. *Style: Toward Clarity and Grace.* 3d ed. Chicago: University of Chicago Press, 1990.

Winkler, Anthony C., and Jo Ray McCuen. *Writing the Research Paper: A Handbook with Both the MLA and APA Documentation Styles.* 4th ed. Fort Worth, Tex.: Harcourt Brace, 1994.

On Style

American Psychological Association. *Publication Manual of the American Psychological Association.* 4th ed. Washington, D.C.: APA, 1994.

The Chicago Manual of Style. 14th ed. Chicago: University of Chicago Press, 1993.

Gibaldi, Joseph. *MLA Handbook for Writers of Research Papers.* 4th ed. New York: Modern Language Association, 1995.

Slade, Carole, William Giles Campbell, and Stephen Vaughan Ballou. *Form and Style: Research Papers, Reports, Theses.* 9th ed. Boston: Houghton Mifflin, 1994.

Turabian, Kate L. *A Manual for Writers of Term Papers, Theses, and Dissertations.* 6th ed., rev. John Grossman and Alice Bennett. Chicago: University of Chicago Press, 1996.

On Publishing

Luey, Beth. *Handbook for Academic Authors.* 3d ed. New York: Cambridge University Press, 1995.

Index